These poems are "messages from the homeland" of the heart, where Ana Lisa has spent a lifetime exploring pain and beauty, a pain and beauty we intuitively recognize as our own. Poems that make it perfectly all right to feel like "a little scrap of leaf, decaying," because we have fallen "in the sun's endless rising," even if dawn has not quite come. Poems that speak to something primordial and chthonic inside us, our origin, our root: "When you speak to someone/ speak to the tree in them." Poems of solace, grief sharing, quiet joy, and inward light, often propelled by reference to great mystics like Hafez, Rumi, and Hildegarde of Bingen. De Jong's words pour from a deep stream of spirituality whose current gains greater force by echoing ancestral voices. These 'Bodies of Water' taste fresh and clear, yet that taste is infused with the spirit of the ancient masters.

~ **Alfred K. LaMotte**,
author of *The Nectar of This Breath, Wounded Bud,*
and *Savor Eternity One Moment at a Time.*

Enter in. I love these poems of connection, of place, of exploration and opening. At the same time they touch silence and the great song of being. They invoke the body of earth, the human body and the immeasurable body of love. I love the way these poems dance in the mystery, touch what is true, and *turn in a widening circle* to affirm the world that is.

~ **Rosemerry Wahtola Trommer**,
author of *All the Honey* and *Hush*

How can one possibly describe such a gifted, awakened poet as Ana Lisa de Jong? Immersed for many days in her most recent collection, *Bodies of Water,* I've been effortlessly transported into eternity on the wings of an Unknowable Mystery and simultaneously swept into the deepest currents and intricacies of the human Heart.

A sublime merging of imminence and transcendence! "What if reality were the wick from which our life spark is lit?" Ana Lisa asks. Such a marvelous inquiry—a neurological probe to access, open and expand the radiant heart-mind of all who read her words. I bow with deep-abiding respect.

~ **Rashani Réa**, co-author of *go slowly, breathe and smile*, author of *Beyond Brokenness* and *Beneath All Appearances: an unwavering peace*

BODIES OF WATER

By Ana Lisa de Jong

No part of this book may be reproduced, stored in a retrieval system, or transmitted by any means, electronic, mechanical, photocopying, recording, or otherwise without written permission from the author.

Copyright © Ana Lisa de Jong 2023. All rights reserved.

The right of Ana Lisa de Jong to be identified as the author of the Work has been asserted by them in accordance with the New Zealand Copyright Act 1994.

ISBN: Hardcover: 978-1-98-855730-4
ISBN: Softcover: 978-1-98-855731-1
ISBN: Ebook: 978 1 98 855733 5

Published Year: 2023
Published in the United States of America by Three Ravens Media

Table of Contents

Water Cycles xiii

Buoyant. 1

    Buoyant 3
    Breath Rises 5
    Enliven Me 7
    Liberators 9
    Disturbance 11
    Reality 13
    Dark 16
    God Breathed 18
    Inadequate 21
    Faithwalker 23
    Spreading Light 25
    More 27
    Joy As Medicine 29
    Reflection 32
    Grace Of Tree 34
    Waves 36
    Water 38
    Key Holes 41
    Freedom 43
    Perpetual Motion 44
    How Not 46
    Joining The Dots 48
    Now 50
    Te Waikoropupū Springs 52

Under The Mountain **55**
    Above And Under 57
    Beneath 59
    Fiords 61
    Papatūānuku 64
    Spiralling 67
    Under The Blue Sky. 68
    Inside Every Living Being 71
    Signs Of Life 73
    Page Turning 76
    Sandalwood. 79
    Observation 81
    Listening. 83
    Pouring. 86
    Grace As A Well 88
    Hush 90
    Yielding 92
    Mirrors 93
    In The Heart. 95

Bodies Between **97**
    Body Of Water. 99
    What Is Love 100
    Light 102
    Waterfalls 104
    Touch 106
    Diamonds. 108
    Seeing 110
    Moonstruck 112
    Peace Tunes. 114
    Slow 116

Starlight 117
Soft God 118
The Elusive Thing 119
Where Do Our Tears Go 122
When You Speak 124
The Way It Is 127
Rivers 129

Belonging 131

Backbone 133
Belonging 134
Two Seas 136
My Song 140
Heart Strings 142
A House 143
Marriage 144
Colonies 145
The Colour Of Sky 147
Together 150
Weather Systems 152
One Forest 155
Four Seasons In A Day 157
The Middle 160
Your Heart 162
Pilgrims 165
Stars 167
This Close 168
Further 170
Weather Forecast 173
Beauty To Survive 175
Daylight 177

    Ingrained 178

    Tangles. 179

    Hooked. 182

    Earthy Grace 184

    God Kicks 186

    The Word. 188

    Holy Love 190

    Symbiosis. 192

    Islands 194

Islands. 197

    Beyond. 199

    Alone 200

    Dignity 202

    Concessions. 204

    A Leaf 206

    Encircled 208

    Heart Quake 211

    Overcoming. 212

    Gilt Edged 215

    Never Ending. 218

    Around The Sun. 220

    Memory Of Light. 222

    Unknown 224

    Wind Tunes. 225

    Life Is A Poem 227

    Sides. 229

    Travellers 232

    Recalling Eternity 235

    Imagining. 239

    Blooming 242

Hands Free	244
Within	246
Time Tomorrow	249
Reflections At Mt Cook	251
Fire And Ice	255
At The Heart	257
Merton's Cabin	259
The Space Between Notes	262
About the Author	266

This poetry collection is dedicated to Ngāi Tahu,
the principal Māori iwi (tribe) of the South Island,
Aotearoa-New Zealand

'Ko au te awa, ko te awa ko au'
I am the river, the river is me.

— Māori Whakataukī

Dear readers,

Once every now and then we are given to travel. Many of the poems from this book were born out of a family trip to the South Island in May 2022.

Perhaps I had a feeling the poetry composed during our travels would one day make its way into print. On the first night of our travels in Lake Taupo I composed the following in an online post:

As we stay at Lake Taupo tonight, it becomes evident to me that this will be a story of lakes and rivers and of bodies of water. I suspect this poem might be one of many to signify that. I hope you might join me on the journey.

I do hope you join me in the reading of this collection to experience the unique flavor of Aotearoa-New Zealand in the way that its bodies of water, its mountains of grandeur, its still mirror lakes and its rushing rivers speak to us. Also interspersed within this collection are other recently written poems capturing the essence of water, mountain, sky, and all the elements that come to stir our spirits and bring our senses alive when experiencing the natural world.

This collection wouldn't be complete without acknowledging the main Māori iwi (tribe) of the South Island, Ngāi Tahu. When experiencing a place I attempt to be cognisant of the many footsteps already impressed upon the whenua (land) before us—there is a sense of giving homage to those who have called a place home long before us. There is an ancestral presence felt which is both powerful and gracious, in that when we arrive with good intent I believe we are extended 'manaakitanga' (hospitality).

It's also my own Māori ancestral links which help bring the stories and traditions of te Ao Māori (the Māori World) to life for me, and which make the mauri (life essence) palpable in the ngahere (bush), the maunga (mountains), and the moana (ocean).

As the Psalmist has reflected, 'deep calls to deep', and it is when we are stirred by a magnificence beyond ourselves that we also contemplate the evidence of a creator. Henry David Thoreau has said, 'my profession is always to find God in nature'. Certainly, in my poetry God and the natural world are hard to separate from one another, and much of this book is a testimony to the God I see woven through nature, bringing the spiritual to life in the tangible present.

I hope this poetry will speak to those parts of you remembering we are still water, and still air, and still the substance from which we were all derived. Our continuation depending upon the delicate balance of nature, of which we, in all humility and graciousness are welcomed as part of its ongoing story.

Ana Lisa

WATER CYCLES

This is a story of water.
Where water starts and where it stops.
How I have started a journey today,
but was already on it before
I stepped forth.
Like the water that never wasn't.
How before it was river or lake,
it was rain, snow,
precipitation falling
in the great water cycle.

Tonight, I read of Lake Taupō
being so large and deep
a water drop takes 11 years to reach
the other side,
to disperse in the Waikato River.
How this is a story of us.
How we might be snow
falling on Mt Tongariro,
to then melt and find its tributaries
to Lake Taupō–nui–a–Tia,
this great cloak of Tia.
To then again, be churned and mixed
in rapids and waterfalls.

How it isn't always clear of what
we are a part:
lake, river, or rain cloud.

But what is clear is who we are,
and what we are made of,
this H2O we all melt down to.
How we, just like water, are part sky,
and earth and mountain,
part everywhere we've been
and all we survey.

How I start on this journey today
to realise, eternal witness,
what's older than me,
but of which I am made up too.
Thus, I haven't started the journey,
have just picked up with new awareness
my place in it.
No wonder I look at you, water,
and feel as old as you.
Some kinship turning in me somersaults
like water circling.

BUOYANT

BUOYANT

I will build this day from the sky down.

That way I will remember,
I am made of both
the brown earth and stardust.

I will be like the pines
poking my head into the blue.
And will drape the clouds over my hair,
turn my face to the sun.
Sit, a tree dressed in summer foliage.

And somehow, when I go to walk
in my memory of light and dust, I will rise,
and in the place between grounded-ness
and escape,
will live out of a calm, still centre.

Yes, I can hear the cyclists passing without pedalling
now they've picked up the momentum to glide.
Whatever I do today,
let me remember the place
I reside between earth and heaven.

The heavy steps of the runner
I can hear descending the hill
has me thinking of exertion,
and how peace is like the buoyant sea
hardly aware of the contours of the sea floor.

It flows in its currents,
billows and moves its body into waves,
following one after another on to the shore.

What would it be like today to be a wave
powered at its centre?

I shall try all the ways I can
to enact the recollection of my identity
as a part of nature,
with all her graces ready at my disposal.

I shall be like the bird remembering flight,
or a drop of seawater, her body.

BREATH RISES

Breath rises
as incense.

Everything grounded is finite.
This chair, this bed.
This earthbound perception.

But breath rises
as our chests open out,
as our exhales loosen the weight of gravity.

Everything in us
that would hold us firm,
feet submerged,

does not equate to the breath
that weighs nothing
and keeps us alive.

Breath rises,
and we are children at the precipice
trusting in the infinite.

Swimmers, given buoyancy
by the air in our lungs
as much as the salt in the sea.

Breath rises,
and so shall we alight
as wind-borne feathers—

with everything else fallen away
what hold has gravity?

Between God and the soul there is no between.

— Julian of Norwich

ENLIVEN ME

Ah, I gulp fresh air
as though it were made of life,
which it is.

Our limbs may sink,
but it's in the heart reaching out in its need
that we find strength.

Today I am given oxygen
that even sore limbs may still stretch,
find their feet.

I gulp, that the kick-start to the heart
might cause my blood to flow,
enliven me.

There is no need I think
that does not have its medicine,
if not to heal,

at least to help in recuperation
and the easing of recurrent pain.

And this breath

does not need permission to draw.
Since we must breathe to live,
why not deeper?

Why not the extra minutes at the fount of life?
Today it might mean the difference between
sinking or swimming.

And the heart feels a friend as the lungs inflate:
in, out.

That it follows in its motion.
And our feet too, step by step.

LIBERATORS

Have you ever thought of yourself
as a red sea opening?
Have you ever seen yourself as a bridge,
a strip of dry sand, a path
through rolling waves.
A person with their hand up,
for whom the seas subside.

Have you ever thought of yourself,
lying worrying upon your bed,
as a reservoir of answers.
A receptacle of creative thought,
that you might dip your hand in,
come up with a new idea.
A prophet of sorts even.
Someone who gives hopes
new meaning,
fresh clothes.

I think too, as I'm tempted to succumb
to fears,
how the sea is a deep, wide place,
a blue, green, body of currents
flowing in unknown directions.
And I, (although a piece of flotsam) am
someone guided by the heavens,
given a gift of navigation.

And before I sink I stop myself.
Remind myself of the wisdom
of the deep that doesn't depend
on foreknowledge,
just gives itself up to the rolling
momentum.
A body that trusts in passages
and time's unveiling.
How a river marking its way through
a mountain chain,
carving a path over aeons,
teaches us patience.

Ah, that freedom is our inheritance,
and we are a resource in its implementation,
is so easily forgotten when the
waves are breaking.
But we are walking on water witnesses,
we are disciples given purpose
and passion,
and holy imagination.

We are roads in the laying,
and a people made for swimming,
moving, keeping our heads high,
attentive.
Curiosity did not so much kill the cat
as ensure it nine lives for living.
We are a people with answers
and keys to our own liberation.

DISTURBANCE

If I were a leaf, today would be my fall day.
A forest, my mist covered mountain.
And if I were a sea I would stretch out,
keep the waves at bay,
make of myself a smooth lake.

Some days any sound
is the sound of glass breaking.
Any engagement, an intrusion.
And even silence as a sought retreat
can echo out of nowhere—

ricocheting with the sound of stones
or running feet on pavements.

So that I must focus,
take my eyes and seek what they
might grip to, an anchor in the sea.

The magnolia across the street,
size of a dinner plate, that even from here
I can see its petals curled,
its wide, open face,
its supporting leaves.

The white of light reflected,
it's shaking in the breeze.
After which a fantail starts up

its morning serenade,
the cicadas, a background chorus.

And I decide
a falling leaf is what I can be,
afloat on wind currents.
How the winds are picking up now,
the magnolia bloom hardly batting her petals,
the branches bearing the weight of each gust.

How the deck roof is creaking,
and the palm trees, scraping their fronds.
While I, sitting here still,
are a quiet lake in a gale,
a leaf unattached
and settled on a forest floor.

Come move me, shake me, I might say,
and I will answer undisturbed.
What power there is in relinquishment,
not unlike silence and its
up and down voice,

its bidding into life's circus,
in the shelter of its hand.

REALITY

We are tied to this body, that is all.
Tied by the matter of a mind
and heart contained.

But there is something in us
that is not of the physiology of cells and molecules,
or the function of muscles and organs.

There is another something in us
that science might research and try to explain,
and fall short.

Feeling and thought,
the internal mechanisms
of an ever moving engine room in which we process reality,
cannot explain it—

the 'what else' beyond our minds and hearts,
the nugget of us.

What if our reality
were not the earth under foot,
or the skin over flesh,
or the extent of our vision?

What if reality were the wick
from which our life spark is lit,
the thing in us ever arising
and defying the confines of our being?

Which enables us to understand Jack Gilbert
when he says: we are not the lake,
nor the fish in it, but the 'something'
that is pleased by them.

We are not the big maple, but the wind
through its leaves.

And how we are certainly not our body,
although we use it to make music.
We are the something that hears it
and responds.

Our life is all grounded and rooted in love,
and without love we may not live.

— Julian of Norwich

DARK

When the night has sighed her last breath,
lain down as foliage in a diminishing wind,
surrendered to the day's closing curtain,

we see her dense as a forest,
dark as the backs of eyelids,
and remember how
to float on the sea takes a certain trust
and immersion in the midst of nothing—

just the weight of water and a carpet of stars,
our arms and a world turning silent circles.

The night has a certain authority
in her quiet stance,
all our complaints echoing out,
with little choice but to leave undone
everything the day has not enabled,
to accept the words misfired, left unuttered,
fallen short of any mark.

For sleep to come we observe the dark,
how everything is swallowed whole.
How like compost it works its slow alchemy
turning leftovers to newly made life.

That in the day, when the sun is restored,
we find the light brings a full new wick.
Which we, yawning, carry and light.
Our every breath a new formed wonder.
Our every hope like a person drowning,
who found that water could bear him up.

Yes, who would believe that under night's dark coverage
our strength once spent could be fully recovered.
Yes, to float on the sea takes a certain trust
and immersion in the midst of nothing—

just the weight of water and a carpet of stars,
our arms and a world turning silent circles.

GOD BREATHED

If you are a twig, you are the twig of a tree.
If you are a wave, you are a wave rising from an ocean.
If you are a ray of light, your source is the sun.
Though you might only know yourself
a slim finger illuminating the undergrowth.
If you are here, then you are life inhabited.
If you are here, you are doing more
than swimming in air, inhaling the elements.
And sometimes forgetting,
as John O'Donohue has said,
how strangely wonderful we all are in being.

Not one of us arriving here by ourselves,
just like this condensation on the window pane,
lit brilliant in the dawn's light.
You might call God life
and you could not be more accurate.
No dead deities here.
From the edges of our consciousness
we might be aware of a loving source
giving us all strength for living.

Do you think a drop of ocean
has full knowledge of its inherited magnificence?
All it knows is it is somehow held afloat,
given leash to ride upon the breast of waves,
be carried by currents.
We too are not long birthed from the womb,

holding the memory of dark
and its surrounding fluids.
We were there,
and now we're here.
But the invisible umbilical cord waving in the
wind is our connection to origins.

And the air,
is a reminder we are sustained,
the ocean, a reminder
we are larger than our singular selves.
The earth, a reminder we are
greening spring trees,
that in our seasons we shed
and blossom and disperse.
So that even breaking down we are
transforming,
our energies harvested for a forest.
Do not forget then, if you are twig,
you are tree.
If you are tree, you are part of
this copse of bush
running down to the ocean
helping a planet breathe.

Oh, how we give God a name, or a gender,
and we think we're closer.
But she is like the firefly darting into the night,
or a heaven illuminated with pinpricks of stars,
that we are exhausted in the counting.
So next time you think of God,
or wonder about yourself, don't doubt,
or even attempt to gain a grasp upon it—
this wonder in being.

Smile and gaze upon yourself in the mirror,
and see how the blue of your
eyes reflect the skies of the heavens.
The wonder of you, fully evident,
though it might not bear the counting.

INADEQUATE

We feel so inadequate sometimes
to bring a light to ward off the dark.

We are powerless to push aside
its breadth and height, its creeping edge.

We feel alone, that even together we must
reach for each other's hands,

walk one careful step,
one hard day at a time.

Yes, we feel overwhelmed,
undone.

That the dark, sometimes like water
tempting our immersion—

with its great body to envelop
and carry us to oblivion—

can seem a thought easier
than our burdens.

But to feel afraid perhaps,
is our signal to reach for hands of support,

for helpers holding gentle
torches in the night.

Yes, there is nothing that need be dealt with
alone.

And that is the light,
the light that sends the darkness to its knees.

How it only takes one candle
meeting another,

and the flame of love carried across a room,
to light up all the cavernous corners.

Shadows, only spectres we have not faced,
turned our lights upon.

FAITHWALKER

Oh faith walker,
with the broken stride,
the stumbling step,

how much do you pray without knowing,
live by faith though it seems
at times a lantern dim?

And your feet,
how often do they discern their way
with hope and trembling trust?

And your hands,
that press forward as a swimmer in the sea,
how often do they feel ahead, navigating their way?

Oh faith walkers each,
how often do we pray?

It may not be in sentences,
with questions or pleas,
or even praises.

Sometimes hope is such a small seed,
that to keep it hidden in the dark
where it can germinate is a quiet feat.

And praise can seem a risk before the full signs of spring,
so that our hearts may only speak
in breath prayers of longing.

But what is prayer?
Is it only real if another hears us,
or if we can hear ourselves make sense of speech?

And what are words?
But a language given for communication
for those with ears.

While between us and God there isn't need
for words or expression,
and nothing less than a deep deep sea

with untold currents moving.

SPREADING LIGHT

My friends have gone back to
spreading light.
Just when I thought I would
have to close this book.
Turn myself into a round stone,
a chrysalis waiting
for a passage of time,
a deep-water fish
needing darkness.

But my friends have turned
like restless
sleepers in the night,
have sought unconsciously
for the sun's appearance,
have shaken themselves
like the newly woken,
have reached like the thirsty
for pitchers of water.

And my friends have gone
back to spreading light.
Just when I thought I might
quietly bow out.
Turn myself into a monk
in remembrance
of Thich Nhat Hahn
and the ways of peace—

of Thomas Merton,
his wilderness cabin,
a haven in a storm

While my friends,
my friends,
were already ahead of me,
watching intently
for Matariki dawning,
casting nets.

MORE

To do, when you want more:

Sit down and feel the ground.
Feel how it is moving and not moving.
Breathe and feel your lungs,
how they expand and contract without your notice.
Know that more is as much waiting for you
as you are looking for it.
It may seem like little is happening
but for the tide, coming in and out.
It may seem like little is moving
but you going around in circles.
But perhaps that is the way of momentum,
the planet on its axis,
the moment on its cusp.
Sit there and let more fall into your lap,
splashing
as the juice of the watermelon
split open.
That its hard roundness
contains such sweetness within
is always a surprise.
Somehow like the moment
tapping us on the shoulder,
reminding us how it is all there is.

When anxious, uneasy and bad thoughts come, I go to the sea,
and the sea drowns them out with its great wide sounds,
cleanses me with its noise, and imposes a rhythm upon everything
in me that is bewildered and confused.

— Rainer Maria Rilke

JOY AS MEDICINE

Joy too often feels like a luxury
that we should go without
for the sake of our neighbours.
There is too much pain and loss
and terror in the world
to be joyful in the face of it.
How entitled are we to still claim it?

And sometimes joy, overly nurtured,
feels like a hot house flower we've
transplanted with care,
only for it to turn up its heels
at the first touch of frost.

And yet joy, I feel her,
so tenacious and
ever-appearing.
While I struggle with doubts
or confidence,
or guilt (valid or not)
or despair even, when looking
in various directions,
joy tells me it's only weather.

That joy is the plant rooted in bedrock,
unmoved and spreading seeds.
Or the bird in its nest of trees,
watching the storms pass overhead,

assessing when it's safe
to re-emerge.
And doesn't joy arrive again then,
like a flock of seagulls on the shoreline
watching us eat,
excited for crumbs.

Yes joy, I think, is like a drop
of vivid dye,
and we pilgrims
at the lakeside
looking in mirrors.
Doesn't joy dare us
to hurry up and take out the vial.
How it takes just a smidgen to turn
the green waters blue.

Oh joy, thank you!
How you come running like a child
at his father's re-appearance.
The child who has already forgotten
the argument of the morning,
or hasn't perhaps,
and hating how it feels
is just intent now on restoration.

Oh yes, joy who knocks us over,
come running full tilt toward us.
Help us right the world a little bit
with your serious frivolity.
How we feel stronger again for letting you in,
as new air in the lungs,
revived with purpose and meaning.

And this blossoming world
built on last year's remains,
how it ever reflects you,
how it's we who are in need
of our eyes opened.

Mary Oliver,
who said joy was not a crumb,
I believe knew it takes love received
to know what love is
and to be capable of spreading it.
And it takes joy,
even if just a smidgen,
to cleanse the whole vision.
Joy, this medicine of nations.

REFLECTION

What needs to go?

What like the seasons is preparing to shed,
or to grow,
is silent yet in the earth?

To reflect,
make three columns
with your paper and ink:

then walk
through the garden of your life
with full attentiveness.

Take part in your practice
with your arms raised
like the trees,

that you might feel the praise of
sap running through fingers,
the budding at their tips.

Then close your eyes and feel
what falls in a rustle of leaves,
the release of weight.

And pay attention as you walk
to see where weeds need clearing
that the earth might breathe

and seedlings emerge,
what plants need space to spread
and flourish.

Feel the earth and thank her
for her storage of the secret
things still to sprout.

And for the sacred place she
makes for everything fallen
to break down and become new mulch.

And see the sky and sun
shining golden through new leaves.
And know how

in heaven our gardens are prepared,
that here is a reflection
as the waters of a lake

mirroring the morning,
all blue and green
in the clearing mist.

And remember, you have all the seeds
for these gardens,
for which we have been given the vision

for creating, for nurturing
in the endless cycles of the seasons,
heaven nodding in affirmation.

GRACE OF TREE

When the leaves fall
do you think the tree wonders
what is happening,
giving herself up to the cold?

When the camellias
drop their white petals
as a carpet to be trodden over,
rained upon,

do you think the shrub
asks who made her bloom
for a season,
to then divest her of her wealth,
her flush hand?

Do you think nature sighs,
takes a deep angst-filled breath,
asks the plan
for this change of path,
unexpected diversion?

Or is there in the apparent
patient grace of tree,
of blooming short-lived faces
of flowers,
a prior understanding,
an acknowledgement of the fragility
of being?

That recognises the
wider web of life
and how each
small role supports
the whole,
the overarching intent
for preservation,
for continuance.

Just like the spider
weaving her daily house,
having had it blown down,
brushed away
by a careless hand,
starts again.

WAVES

I have watched the waves
beat their way to the shore,
counting
35 long seconds of cresting
and rolling before
breaking upon the sand.

And I wonder,
standing here looking down,
and numbering my years in scores
and tens,

whether the wave knows
its rolling, cresting weight
will break upon the shoreline
to retreat again.

To become reabsorbed into ocean
and its churning heaving mass.
The wave having had
its 35 seconds of fame,

its moment in the spotlight
of the moon.
After which it is part again
of a body giving shape

to new waves
and journeys on the surface,
rolling and cresting
and shattering in the face of the sun.

And I wonder if we realise
all our human strength
and illusioned might,
is propelled by a force under us.

And like the wave we crest
and crash
with nothing to fear
but the embrace of an ocean beneath.

WATER

Wendell Berry tells me to sit.
It seems the antithesis,
the converse of what I should be doing.

I sit wringing my hands,
feel my heart beating too strong.
There is everything I wish to change.

Wendell Berry says that in the time of no rain
we are to sit and wait
until we hear it running over stone.

In this dry season something
is sustaining my leaves
or I would break, from brittleness.

There must be a spring somewhere,
a well beneath me.
I don't know, I am all leaf

buffered by the things I cannot change,
or move, or alter,
cause to come to fruition.

Sometimes I wish I were the wind
or the rain,
the weather with its power to affect things.

But Wendell Berry reminds me,
as does Merton
and Mother Mary,

all coming through to me
in the dry whirl,

that I am not the world,
but only someone with a small role
in its solution.

And mine, I think sometimes,
is to sit statue still
until I can hear a squall one thousand miles distant,

the coming change of season,
a source of water.

So that while everyone is scurrying
I can be a bearer of possibility,
of renewal,
pointing to the heart and head,

smiling and gesturing
toward something unseen,
that they might hear it too,

this running calm in the centre.

And might know themselves as fuelled
by a source that doesn't stop its
springing forth,

despite circumstances,
despite everything as it is
appearing dead

and in need of resurrection.

In the dark night of the soul, bright flows the river of God.

— St John of the Cross

KEY HOLES

There is a tear in the firmament
under which the earth resides.

Breathes,
lungs falling, rising.

We are like people visiting a lakeside,
who see our reflection in the water
and God beyond.

And God is the father
whose daughter has departed,
is building her own life.

But who knows there is a gap
in the keyhole,
and a curtain she leaves ajar for him,

too afraid that on her own
she will veer off track,
unknowing.

She does not want his opinion
necessarily,
or any obvious resemblance to his traits,

but she needs the knowing,
in every cell of her own being,
that she is cared for,

not forgotten.

And God knows one day,
when she parents,
she will speak in her father's voice.

There is a tear in the firmament
through which God loves
at just the right distance.

That we are not alone
but independent,
and in some rare moments aware

of an encompassing,
unsurpassing love.
Somewhat like a breach of defences.

And we are people at a lakeside
contemplating our reflections,
seeing God behind.

Breathing in, out,
resting assured.

FREEDOM

I don't know,
I think I must follow the sky.

Is there a reason the trees point upwards,
and the ocean rolls in blue waves
mimicking the clouds?

Perhaps when everything seems impossible
and circumstances restrict,
the sky,

shining there
as a parable put in front of us,
is the very promise we need guaranteed.

Our freedoms assured
in the way she says 'look at me',
and in how she can't be corralled.

The way she is still there when we turn around
that we can't not be covered,
as well as inspired.

Even when we spin until we're dizzy,
and lie out spread-eagled on the grass,
she is there

whipping out her blankets
for catching falls.

PERPETUAL MOTION

The sun doesn't falter.
Does not need a few moments to withdraw
and collect herself.

Not that rest is wrong,
but she could not stop her shining
if she tried.
And the earth, in its motion does not slow
its revolving
and its forward momentum.

Does not take its time to think:
today I might take it easy.
It has too many dependent
on its continued trajectory.

Like the sun,
who could not step back from her station
without a humanity's collapse.

Instead the sun and earth, and moon,
the natural world,
everything in nature,

other than us perhaps,

know how to carry with them, rest
as a shell on their back,
a calm centre in the whirl.

That we too, in their midst,
are moving with little awareness of it.
But still make our own whirlwinds,
tornados of feelings and action,
that sometimes we're pulled up short,
out of breath,

and in awareness of all those dependent on us.

The sun doesn't falter in her brightness,
the world in its turning within her beams.

Perhaps it's the light that keeps the earth
in its perpetual motion.
Might we lasso it, that it be our reason.

HOW NOT

I want the joy that does not depend
on happiness,
fed as it is by inner springs.

The joy that aches at the edge,
only to make it the more intense,
profound.

I want joy as streams
running through canyons,
cascading upon the dry earth.
Joy, that when you asked its reason,
would say, 'how not?'
'How not joy?'

As in,
can we climb the looming hill
without water in our packs?

Who of us would set forth on a long walk
unprepared?
Though on the path we'll shed things.

In the end we might see that many things
we thought we needed,
we didn't.

But not joy.

Joy, like oil on the bicycle's chain,
or Vaseline on blistered feet,
the drink by the fire after a day's pilgrimage.

We all need the joy
that bookends the day,
can be found at every lay-by and watering hole.

Yes, I have a glass I carry
no-one can see,
except perhaps upon my countenance.

And I am always checking
it's at least half full.
That if not, I'll veer from the path for refreshment.

For if I were a tree, I would die
if my sap were to harden,
run itself dry.

Yes, I want the joy that does not depend
on happiness,
fed as it is by inner springs.

The joy that aches at the edge,
only to make it the more intense,
profound.

Joy as streams
running through canyons,
cascading upon the dry earth.

Joy, that when you asked its reason,
would say, 'how not?'

JOINING THE DOTS

How to build a bigger circle?
Join the dots: A, B, C.
Come back changed,
to find everything is smaller than before.
Then go again.

Go round again in your mind.
See if you can fill it out.
Take a deep breath,
the mountain air,
the lakes, metres deep.

Don't speed, don't move home
until you can float.
Then expand,
taking with you sweep of sky,
snow from a southern slope,
water droplets scooped.

Then jump in leaps and bounds.
Until, hop, you have jumped into home.
Never fear—now lift the roof,
remembering the stars.

Block your ears,
to hear the water rushing.
There ıs a larger circle
around the one you've drawn.
You made it all yourself.

The way you've thrown out your arms,
spun in every direction.
You've expanded your map,
made your journey hitherto different.

Now when people ask you
where you've been,
you will get that faraway look in your eyes,
and join the dots to circle again.

NOW

It is where you are now
which is the only thing true,
the only thing that matters.

That you can sink into the pillow,
or the sand, or the green grass
and turn your head

that the sun will make a beam
right upon your face,
or the gracious dark.

The hills are both in sun and shadow
from where I am now,
and the mountains

have made a cradle of the lake
as deep as they are high,
with us somewhere afloat
in the middle.

And the sun does her full tilt
from slope to slope,
indifferent and yet positioned

so that we are neither too hot, nor cold,
as though somehow
to be given the requirements for life
is enough.

For what else does the rose
need to bloom,

and what does it know but the moment,
stretched at its highest point
as a golden dome of light,
to then sink as a stone in the cradle of the dark.

The golden leaves here
make a folly of the need to know.
That we must always chase the light
is a ruse the hurried fall ever into.

We know, roots in the ground or bodies afloat,
that the sun will make her way around,

and the moment dissolve into light,
flickering as a flame from wick to wick,
now reducing to embers

to then reignite.

TE WAIKOROPUPŪ SPRINGS

The forest is breathing.
I walk through its fresh air,
a cool, light mantle settling,
the wairua of the forest enveloping me.
This, I whisper to myself,
is a sacred place,
to stop, linger,
release for healing all,
that like the dancing springs,
or the rushing stream,
surfaces,
becomes a need in me to get up and walk
to the altar of my being,
to meet at the source,
the giver of life.

This, I whisper, is a place of purity,
the very air ringing with
an ancient clarity.
The green of the trees bordering
the blue springs,
an untouched Eden.
This sacred place
of the thinnest of parchments,
like a slip of wafer paper
folded next to heaven,
all distance an illusion.

The truth being,
as water deep and clear,
that the blessing is springing
everywhere,
and we, moving as reeds,
or blue, green reflections
in a lake transparent,
hardly know we are vessels
immersed in heaven.

UNDER THE MOUNTAIN

ABOVE AND UNDER

Above and under the mountain
is still mountain.
We kneel at the mid-point
beside the lake,
contemplating the reflected hills
and trees.

How each requires the other:
subject and reflection.
Just as under the mountain
is still mountain.

And above the lake are trees.
Yes, stop now.
Stop right here and see how
we are stones battered and polished.
Stop right now and see how
we are surrounded by earth and sky.

That I take all my angst,
even that gathered since
leaving the lakeside,
my future fears and current concerns,
and in my mind throw stones.

Plop, I hear them hit and sink down
beneath the quiet tree lined pond.

And then stand to walk,
hills and mountains in my vision,
unchanged.

'Wait', I call to whoever's gone ahead,
'I'm coming.'

Now lighter in weight.
That now I pray to keep it so.
What a memory this lake will be in my vision.
That and the mountains behind.

BENEATH

There is a place that lies there hidden,
quiet beneath
the cacophony of life.

Like the hue of green,
which although predominant
has its shades of light and dark,

and underneath, a canvas blank,
its colour just a reflection of light.

So everything on the surface,
the buzz and business of the world,
hides behind it.

A vastness stretched
as a prairie in the evening sun,
or desert sweeping to infinity,

empty of much but the endless sky,
quiet as an encompassing womb.

That we might spend our whole lives
looking and evading
this quiet mirror,

the still length of unfurled cotton,
this blueprint
of our wide-eyed self.

The place that in all our living
we have left as a discarded shell.

Many of us spend our whole lives running from feelings
with the mistaken belief
that you cannot bear the pain. But you have already borne the pain.
What you have not done is feel all you are, beyond that pain.

— Kahlil Gibran

FIORDS

Wander where
the heart
has room
to branch.

How we are fiords
for the tides
to move through.
Spread fingers
of a body opening up
for the sea.

At the bottom
of the world,
where we are most ourselves,
there is no pretence,

no scaffolding
against the blinding light
of the sun through
low cloud.
The mist that clears
to reveal a luminous world.

The depths of ourselves
created by glacial movement
over time.
Melting to leave behind
fissures for oceans to fill.

How we are both height and depth.
And those who travel our waters,
witnesses of mysteries
too profound
to understand.

Yes, might we know ourselves
as many fingered,
branching hearts,
with endless room,
deep and high.

With bush clad hills,
straight sided cliffs,
waterfalls,
and depths of darkness
where the weight of water
forms a shield

for the heart wide open,
its many fissures
and access points,
entries for pain and rapture both.

How we are to live
like the spread-eagled fiords,
hospitable to light
and ocean,
open to beauty,

and the way that light cuts a path
to the quick,
that we are less surprised
than gratified.
Less shy than held in awe
of ourselves,

caverns for a moving sea.

PAPATŪĀNUKU

When God lay down,
he took her with him,
Papatūānuku

That flesh became a bed for grasses.
And the grooves and hollows,
lakes and rivers.

And the hills,
inclines gently shaped
and rounded as the curve of cheek,
of breast.

And the mountains
thrust up
as arcing backs
in a spasming rush of love,

before lying prone,
knotted spines against
a horizon.

And when Papatūānuku stretched,
languid after love,

she sent her arms
as wings out into the ocean,
drawing peninsulas of light and storm.

Waved her fingers
into long green fiords,
made of her flesh a carpet
for a wilderness

of flora and fauna
to the shoreline:
nīkau green and rata red,
kauri and tōtara tall.

Her summer cloak
a wreath of feathers, and snatches of song:
huia, kōkako,
korimako.

Her winter down soft
in its blue white snow-capped fringes,
and silver fingered rivers,
tussock edged.

Yes, when God lay down
he drew her close,
Papatūānuku.
Too beautiful to lose.

Peopled her flesh,
that the outpouring from her womb
would fill the plains and valleys,
echo with the sounds of children.

For God is a lover first,
tethered to his creations.
And we, birthed from the darkness
of the whare tangata

into the world of light,
are children of Papatūānuku,
the Earth Mother,
and God both.

SPIRALLING

Enter in.
So far you see the passageways within.
When you don't know where to go
but round in circles,
you see how everything in life
is spiral.
We are sometimes whisked into the air
like planets spinning,
but even they are on their
vortex trajectory.
There is order in the chaos
unperceived by our short sightedness.
Trust then in the gaping hole
at every entrance.
We are a mollusc in a shell
longing for home,
while living in its curved
sanctuary.
Though we feel ourselves
at the mercy of the ocean currents,
we are adrift upon the mystery
of the Great Wisdom.
Not lost and not without
ways forward.
Though we turn, and we pivot
and we somersault,
while falling we are learning
how to fly.

UNDER THE BLUE SKY

Under the blue sky are the green trees,
grown taller and wider in the spring,
that living now is in a hammock
strung beneath a soft canopy.

And under the green trees is the earth,
rich and fertile,
an undergirding of the garden growing up and out.
A seed bed for its continuing.

And under the soil is the rock enduring,
a foundation stone upon which we live and spin.
And under the rock again,
is earth, sky and trees,
and ocean, desert, mountains.

Life on every surface of a planet
moving at speed,
while at rest still in unseen hands.

And under the blue sky
is a dark space extended,
punctuated by bright specks of stars,
within which is our galaxy, revolving,
drawing us forever on.

And above is blue sky,
and green trees grown taller
and wider in the spring,
and above again,
the stars and the planets,

that living now is in a hammock
made up of galaxies
threaded with stars and planets,
strung between two outstretched hands.

Of all that God has shown me,
I can speak just the smallest word,
Not more than a honey bee
takes on his foot
from an over spilling jar.

— Mechtild of Magdeburg

INSIDE EVERY LIVING BEING

You did not know God was inside you.
How you felt like a tree
whose leaves had grown old,
brittle from summer sun and winds,
from too much time standing.

You did not know God was inside you.
This shape-changing master of disguise,
who takes himself so seriously
as to immerse himself
in the objects of his affection.

You did not know God was so quiet.
Invisible even, until in the Autumn seasons,
deciding to come out
in blazes of vibrant colour,
in revelatory displays.

How God always moves without footprints,
stands without words
in the corners of crowded rooms,
witnesses the forgetting of ourselves,
bides his time.

How you did not know God was inside the living,
revealed in the broken.
Luminous,
like the night sky
cracked open with stars.

How every in-breath is a beginning of God,
every exhalation, a remembrance.
Every leaf that turns from brown to gold,
to red,
falls,

an out-working of the inner creative force
that has set up house.
Is ever making something new
out of something,
eternal alchemist.

How you did not know God existed, hidden,
or otherwise known by countless other names.
How you did not know that God
was the one within,
loving, hoping,
entrusting you with dreams.

God as an island, a fertile spring soil.
A garden, abounding in blossom,
bringing the birds.
How you hardly knew God was in the seasons,
until he was.

SIGNS OF LIFE
—*Thoughts while listening to Thomas Merton*

Underneath, trust for seeds.

Under the rustle of the forest mulch
and last year's life,
the dark earth holds its beating heart.

Its lungs that breathe consistently,
unheeding surface stresses,
following the earth's natural rhythms.

Trust too in the seeds in others.
Under the baggage of accumulated griefs,
hopes dashed, insecurities,

is the pulse of life, prodding, pushing,
seeking outlets for new fresh growth.

Trust too in the rhythms of the universe,
the pull of the moon upon the oceans.

All of nature, of which we are a part,
demonstrates to us the instinct
for life's continuance

against the odds,
and because of them.

And know too that we are free
in the flowing streams of life.

Sometimes what holds us stationary
are things we're resistant to surrendering.

Reeds we grasp at as we pass,
unaware of the flourishing growth
around each river's bends.

So, know your place in everything,
that you do not need to fight to keep.

The dance master is always holding out his hands,
making us room upon the dance floor.

It is not survival of the fittest,
so much as survival of the whole.

And the whole depends on our roles within it,
that when we fall someone will replace us.

Not through substitution,
but such as a forest sparks
from leaf to leaf in one large fire.

Yes, underneath are the seeds of continuance.

That when fear strikes we take our garden forks,
dig for confirmation of life's returning,
know our places into perpetuity.

I am coming to the conclusion
that my highest ambition
is to be what I already am.

— Thomas Merton

PAGE TURNING

The dark is a page turned,
a light dimmed,
a message to us burning
our candles at each end.

The dark, a way of saying,
'enough of today.'

Everything now given
its equal chance
in the day's light.

Now with night we don't
so much weigh up,
as absolve.

We are a people perceiving
patterns,
falling in the deep dream sleep
of intuition.

The real learnings,
life-long.
And the days,
our practice sessions.

It does not matter
that we are slow at perceiving.
We have time.

And it's not
a series of evening run-downs
of our trip-ups,
and our achievements.
It's more a closing of the curtains.

A winter hibernation.
A sitting, like monks
at the lakeside
watching stones sink,
plop, in the pond.

Waiting for the surface
to clear,
for meaning to be discerned.
Not through straining,
but through patience.

Which is why perhaps
the night,
in this long winter's solstice
of an evening,
seems more drawn out
than the day's light.

Perhaps that is how it is meant,
this inky velvet black,
this cold preserving air
with its ice-compressed lips.
There is no forcing
anything.

At least not until spring,
when things grow of
their own accord.

Yes, how the night
reflects the seasons,
and the day's light,
the miracle of beginnings.

How the dark now
is a covering,
a coming-ready-or-not,
full stop.

A give it all up
for tomorrow,
when it might weigh the same,

but look a little different,
feel even,
like something
new in the hand.

SANDALWOOD

My friend talks of our heart as a dust bowl,
in which we decide then
if we are our own friend or enemy.
I know yesterday I asked my God
where was the bottom?
It seems we think we've hit the floor
and there's a trapdoor.

Perhaps it's like mining.
The heart is so large
and then someone comes
with a pickaxe and a lantern wanting more,
and talking of treasure
that's not yet seen the light of day.

If there is treasure here,
then that someone with the tools
has more faith in it than I,
my eyes aflame with dust.
Though the heart hurts under the rib cage,
I must believe there is more room in there,
that I am being hollowed out for service.

And for learning how to speak of God
with truth and experience,
of this life and its give-and-take struggles,
until we each subside by the wayside.
Know the release
of giving in and giving up.

How else do lovers receive connection,
but by having the courage to allow an approach,
give permission?
Everything an act of will diminishing,
that we must believe
the man with the tools comes also with salve.

Yes, if we are agents for the Divine,
repositories for intimate exchange,
then we must become hewn guitars
made from Sandalwood,
for the one who's already heard
our music from far off,
has come to unearth it.

OBSERVATION

I have felt a great silence run through me.
So much that my pen hasn't reason to speak.

This is the season of observation,
I find myself thinking,
and even then of losing again the things observed,
in that nothing sticks.

I am made of long strappy leaves,
as the ornamental grasses outside the window's pane
point up straight under rain or sun,
having everything wash off them.

The shifting clouds,
which cannot decide themselves
their weather pattern,
have no effect on their green spheres,
that hardly need to right themselves after wind,

but remain gracefully swaying,
as pan flutes in the air currents.

I would that I were them,
but I know I am too ready to identify myself
with nature,
to read myself into her many testimonies.

Like this green spring onion in its water glass
on the window-sill, with her roots afloat,
and her bulbous flower-seeded head
smiling at me unbidden.

But I am in the season of silence
with nothing sticking.
I can hardly discern my own quietness,
let alone compose a poem
as eloquent as grasses or seed-heads.

Or the growing greenness
of a season turning world,
shaking on her axis,
drawing me out of winter's dormancy,
teasing me with her false spring starts,

undecided.

LISTENING

I hear the silence in the wind.
How the tree's leaves brush
one against another.
I hear the silence
in the cricket's night-time tunes,
remembering the child
who mistook them for the stars singing,
that even now
I will sit still listening to the stars.

I hear the silence in the sudden gusts
that shake my shelter,
the clear call of a night owl,
the vortex made
between the singing stars
and the tree's rustling leaves,
branches uplifted.

That I fall, a musical note,
spun around until all is silent
at the centre,
and I realise what it is I've heard
from the start,
listening to wind and crickets.

This source of sound,
from which all music issues,
this song sheet underpinning

a singing universe.
It is the silence of the womb,
the silence after love,
or before sleep,
when everything present
pivots towards the central peace
from which energy springs.

The silence
to which I'm singing
right now,
circled by stars and
corralled by winds,
listening.

So the darkness shall be the light,
and the stillness the dancing.

— T.S. Eliot

POURING

It is pouring so,
that the earth collects our tears as a midwife.

There is no rain pouring into puddles
that will not find its stream,

divert to where it is needed to nourish
and restore.

There is every season,
and some come in floods and hurricanes,

ever torrential
that we cannot keep up.

Our shelters even,
appearing to tumble in the whirlwind.

But there is the cave,
quiet,

secure as a mother after labour,
in gentle awe of the gifts borne from struggle.

And there is a still voice,
waiting, patient,

expectant for the turbulence to be over,
unmoved by seasons running out their course.

Yes, it is pouring so,
that some of us fear we cannot swim,

cannot traverse an ever-widening channel
broadening at the same extent we stroke.

But somewhere in the confusion
is a lifeline,

a carriage to a sea
in which sorrow is absorbed.

And somewhere in the cave
there is hushed anticipation,

that after the whirlwind
will come a still and audible voice.

GRACE AS A WELL

I think of grace as a well,
a lake fed by underground springs,
and we need not wait for death
to dive in.

We can be submerged now,
so that death is simply a lifting of feet
from the bottom,
a floating into the blue beyond.

And grace here, now,
is how we hide from the world,
cannot be hurt
within grace's coverage.

How we can find the strength to love,
to forget injuries,
when the weight of water
softens blows.

This protective grace,
how we embrace the world,
that anyone stepping into our space,
for good or ill, are cushioned,
falling into love.

The type of love that we're all called to,
surrounding and filling us,
that anything we give now
is simply an outpouring.

How we walk on the earth then,
all grace, and dripping wet.

HUSH

Hush,
it's like climbing back into the womb.
This search for silence.
It's like seeing how everything circles in—
the gulls at dusk,
the tide,
the galaxies,
showing us how to spiral.

Far inwards,
that the slow train wreck
we were becoming is halted,
stopped in its tracks
by the realisation
that pausing,
turning, curling,
is a self-protective arc.

The curling of the turtle
beneath its rib bone shell.
A bird's young tucked
under wings.
The earth journeying
away from the sun.

The horse lying down
before rain,
and the cat purring,

clawing at a warm
rugged up lap.

Hush,
as there is no longer need
of lists,
or counting of regrets,
omissions.
There is only tonight,
the very silence
echoing the void
before the earth was formed.

The silence before the beginning.
And everything is always
readying itself to begin.
Although
it doesn't look like readiness,
and so often
feels more like rest,
or the brushing away of tears.

Or hopes dashed,
reimagined,
tentatively re-establishing themselves
in the dark.
The dark of an earth
full-circling, hanging
and leaving
for a moment,
the sun at her back.

YIELDING

Does your heart hurt?
Have you considered someone might be turning it,
the soil of your being,
that seeds might be spread.

Does your body ache?
Do you consider someone may be stretching it,
that through the birth canal
something new might emerge.

Does your soul feel a weight?
Perhaps it's the sorrow of the world
making its way into fallow ground,
burrowing down

until spring warms the earth
and the hard seeds within
have broken,
transforming to something else.

Yes, can you feel the ache of
change,
the yielding needed for
goodness to be dispersed.

If we can blossom through travail,
then the birds will come
and gather the new seeds
from our painful growth,
spread them somewhere else.

MIRRORS

I think sometimes we are
to make of ourselves a lake
that mirrors the blue.

An eye turned inwards in introspection
can draw us further from the truth,
the light.

When instead we were made to rise
above the murky waters,
the dark cold depths,

to where the clouds make their patterns
in the sky,
transpose them upon the water's surface.

We were never meant to see ourselves alone
entirely,
unless in order to discern our connectedness.

A water drop, though it might reflect
the colours of the whole,
needs its neighbours to make a bow in the sky.

Just as a lake,
moving in unison its fluid body,
stills itself to reflect the stars,

the dancing patterns of a cloud,
the setting sun,
peak of mountain.

So I think we too,
to slake our endless longings
and soothe our churning insides,

might lay ourselves down flat
and smooth,
open our eyes to the sun,

make of ourselves prisms
imaging the whole.

IN THE HEART

God is in the heart of us
as seed, as core.
And we must peel
the orange's skin,
feel the paring knife
and its juice run,
in tears,
in trembling joy,
to feel him within.
To know him, not just as Word
or thought,
but as real as the seed in our mouth,
as the core around which the apple
is formed.
God is in the heart of us
that we are not separate or alone.
For God, in the flesh
where pain is felt,
plants himself and reaches out.

BODIES BETWEEN

BODY Of WATER

You move in water.

The sea that accommodates you,
each other.

You move with the grace of angels
in this body of love.

That does not rush to conquer,
but laps at the feet of your neighbour,

woos him in.

Makes us each
as much

or as little room
as we feel comfortable.

We ever think
we teach ourselves to swim,

whereas perhaps
the body of grace

is what holds us up—

this buoyant weight
in which we gently stroke,

which takes our neighbour in its arms.

WHAT IS LOVE

What is love?

Is it how your head rests under my cheek,
your hair on my skin.

How we both burrow into one another
to look out.

Is it how the
waves break against the shoreline

and everything around us,
the sea, the spirits in the air

clap, clap somehow—
that it sounds

like crashing surf,
like seagulls,

like
'I love you'

said into the wind.

It is love alone that gives worth to all things.

— St Teresa of Avila

LIGHT

Oh light,
that you come find me
where I am
and lay your ribbons around me.

That I believe myself alone
until I see the leaves
and their hues change
at the touch of sun.

I see the sea,
and how the sky
is mirrored in its surface,
its radiance doubled.

And perceive then
how everything touches
everything else.

That even the pine needles
I sit upon,
that were once tree,
are cushioning me.

That I cannot move
through the world
without my own influences upon it
is understood now.

How those around me
are dark green or blue,
to then change hue in my presence.

How I am a still sliver of sea,
who under the encompassment
of another, match the sky
in its changing patterns,
its merging of shades.

A little like this body of water
at its horizon
is now indistinguishable from the heavens.

And I think how the distinctiveness of us each
is a mirage,
when instead we move
in and out of each other
as the tides.

WATERFALLS

Let's stop lying,
that we each step serenely,
tip toeing through the garden.
Head high above the earth and dirt.

Let's stop lying,
that we are anything but what God made us.
Beings in need of passion and light,
sensuous as the night and the wild, wild wind.

Let's stop lying,
that the blood in our veins isn't red,
that it doesn't pulse with need
and rush like a river in flood.

Let's stop lying,
that the earth and all her provision is enough.
That we are not in want of a God
who meets us head-on.

Absorbs the energies
without a channel.
Gives us water flowing,
underneath which we might be satisfied.

Let's stop lying,
that we were made for ordinary living.
That the very thing that turns saint to sinner
and sinner to a luminous being

covered in grace,
is not what we each need,
travelling reckless, lying here
restless upon our beds.

For each of us who turn,
turn like lovers into arms,
the branch toward the wind,
the flower to the bee.

Who know
that at the crumbling of our defences
all our walls are breached,
surmounted by a love unrestrained,

with water for the lips.

TOUCH

I wonder how longing arose
in this physical world
where everything substantial
is looking at us.

In this solidity of space
where I might see you
and touch you,
feel the ground.

I wonder and yet don't.
That it didn't seem
so surprising to learn,
a little late,

that we are really just atoms
that dance,
adept at the sidestep,
the give and take.

The electrons in me
keeping you at a distance
infinitesimal,
but none-the-less real.

The atoms in us
lonely at their nucleus,
having never once
made contact

despite our nerve signals,
our brain's storyline.
The friction that feels
like more than air between.

And yet,
forever leaves us gasping,
wanting,

as though the science were right
and longing were a truth
not just a torment,

a kind of heroic
leaping across the gap.
A falling vaguely short.

DIAMONDS

There is a diamond at the centre of us
where we meet.

In every relationship there grows
something else
that we nurture with each interaction.

It is a glowing heart that beats,
a cluster of pearls in a chain.

It is a forest of song birds
and growth beneath.

It is like my candles on the windowsill
now cradling their flames,

their interlinked glass tiles scattering light.

It is the thing that cements
connections in separation,

or ties them still when nerves are frayed
as a length of knitted scarf.

It is the thing we still pick up and hold
after death or loss has made its visitation.

And other than us, existing separate,
undefined by our togetherness, is made

of the eternal essence of us each,
embedded as a diamond into rock.

A living thing, that if we forget each other
it cannot,

built as it is from the remnants of love.

SEEING

It's not what you look at
but what you see.
Not what you look for
but what is there
ready to be revealed.

Too often our thoughts are
like the cloud covered hills.
And we will avoid the sun
in our face
to keep our stories intact.

But the sun keeps nudging us,
with beauty its calling card.
And if we can bear the softening
she will change our gaze
to see what's true.

So often sight
has more to do with the heart
than the eyes.
Protected as it is by shields
and battlements.

While keeping a light on in the heart
means everything we see
is true.

When the sun is shone upon
our shadows
they lose their power to hurt
and haunt,
dissolving as mist at noon.

MOONSTRUCK

The moon has me by the hand again.
If I were a sea I would lay myself down for her.

If I were the sun I would gaze upon her all alight
in my flame.

If I were the world, I would turn,
turn so slowly, holding her face in my view.

And would seek to banish
the burning flame we each orbit,

and live for the day

my shadow falls across her cheek,
though she ventures out far from me.

Yes, the moon has me by the heart again.
That I am a piece of stardust remembering a collision.

I am an earth drawing into the field of its gravity
everything loved.

I am a sea feeling the eternal pull of my body.

Yes, the moon has me held affixed again,
as she hangs at a distance,

all soft roundness and pink cheeks
reflecting a myriad of sunsets.

And I am just a person looking up,
unseen and moonstruck.

PEACE TUNES

There is always peace somewhere.

Where there is a pool deep
on a mountain plateau,
there is peace reflected
as a mountain-scape in the blue.
There is always peace somewhere.

Where there is a forest green
on the side of the highway,
there is peace in the bird's songs,
their lilting tunes clear as flutes.

There is always peace somewhere.

Where there is lack of certainty,
absence of clarity, assurance,
there is peace outside our windows,
the pink, blue tinged clouds.

Open your rooms.

And let the peace transmit from one
doorway to another.
It is like an orchestra, in which we each
play our instrumental parts

in a soaring musical score

that will reach down to your marrow
and then carry you,
a peaceful presence,
to the next person.

SLOW

Slow, slow it down.
Good things take so much time,
as though time were the gift
and not the things obtained.

Good things are like wine smelt,
savoured,
swirled around, almost to the lip
of the glass,
then running down, down,
round again.

And brought so slowly to the mouth
that the tongue might linger
with the taste,
sip before it swallows
the rich red stream,
feel it warm the heart from inside out.

And good things shine
the way candlelight reflects off curves,
returns its own glow,
dances in the eyes,
the smiles of those who know everything desired
is as good as real.

That in the rush, the rush to harness
the ends of our goals,
we miss the satisfaction of imagining,
of everything in between.

STARLIGHT

Who can decide
on what is lost?
When we sanctify it in the memory,
it is a part of us.

As the stars that do not die,
But instead hang in the sky
as more than remembrance
and a light in the dark—

as a clear and
shining testament
to love.

Who can decide then
on what is gone, or know
what is etched on the heart
or the mind

in vivid inks,
on parchments
safe from decay?

Who can say?

SOFT GOD

Ah, God

that you come settle upon us
as the rain from heaven.

That we can turn up our face
and feel your breath,
a benediction upon our skin.

Although soft as a whisper,
still all encompassing,
as the mist of the morning arriving to kiss the earth.

Ah, God

that in silence you stretch out with us,
as dawn sending its brilliant fingers of colour
across the sky's canvas.

That we wake up with you, walk out with you,
and carry you as the breath
with which we caress our neighbour's cheeks,

and as the sun and the wind,
the rain, which moistens the earth,
softening it with grace.

THE ELUSIVE THING

It is that elusive thing
that moves between
the sky and the earth,
the moon and the silken length of sea.

The trees and their neighbours,
the grasses of the fields,
waving, with their tall fronds,
to the birds.

It is the passage of the Holy,
as the wind's currents
which we cannot see
but still feel their existence.

The Holy anointing
that makes everything significant, poignant,
blesses us each.
This sacredness of life.

And is, in intimacy,

the sweetness between us
that takes up no space,
and moves out of the way as we draw close
to then envelop us.

And is the silence that sinks,
a stone,
into the deep sea of our soul
when we survey a view.

The trees, the birds, the ocean.
The foothills bathed in light.

That there is something in us that
speaks the language of the Holy
and responds,
though we may not know it.

And God said to the soul:
I desired you before the world began.
I desire you now
as you desire me.
And where the desires of two come together
there love is perfected.

— Mechthild of Magdeburg

WHERE DO OUR TEARS GO

Where do our tears go,
once they're shed?

Where does our life go
when lived,
and our love after sharing?

Love,
which is the water of life,
where does it dissipate?

Is it simply water in a wheel turning,
converting feeling to energy,
intent to action?

Harnessing its power.

And then,
where does it dissolve
when its gift is fully given?

Where then?

Where do our tears go,
our smiles, our castles built of air,
desires and meanings—

where the gift given

appears simply
as mist evaporating?

Or breath upon the skin —
goose-bump stuff, like cool
puffs of wind

or formless feelings.

Where then?

Where does anything go,
in this world of our singular selves
among billions.

Where we see the rains falling
and the clouds reforming,
full of vapour returned.

And the seasons changing,
the forest growing
upon its own remains,

as though it knows
what it is it has to do.

As though it's some natural law
that nothing is lost,
and everything is transformed.

So, where do our tears go,
or that kiss upon your cheek
that met the air?

Yes, where?

WHEN YOU SPEAK

When you speak to someone,
speak to the tree in them,
remind them of its bending in the wind.

And when you speak,
when it's hard and words are falling to the ground
repelled,

speak to the rock in them,
the protective dignity that keeps them standing ground
in the midst of a roiling sea.

That rock,
though it might ward you off,
is the security from which they draw their strength.

Honour it,
and come and go at their invitation.

And when you speak,
are speaking to the pain in someone,
remember they may curl in for protection,

like the snail or the porcupine,
the turtle with its rigid shell.
Speak gently then,

knowing acknowledgment
goes sometimes much farther
than attempts to fix.

And listening,
even just to the sound of another breathing,
says everything we need it to about solidarity.

And when you speak and must retreat for barbs,
pull them from your soft flesh
and perceive them curiously.

Try not to take offence but seek to understand
by first recognising your own pride
and fears.

And when you speak to someone,
remember the gift of holy listening,
the sacred role of witnessing.

Not changing, making, insisting,
but practising the faith that people are their own
changemakers, rebuilders.

So when you speak to them,
speak to the seed,
and to the flowers you see blooming,

those in bud and about to open.
And remind them of their garden,
of its beauty and bounty.

And when you speak,
remember you cannot see the yeast
when it's mixed into the dough,

but remember the parables
of the kingdom,
and place your trust in the rising.

THE WAY IT IS

See everything the way it is.
Easily said I know,
but try,
and you might make a fair attempt.

Focus in,
and you may no longer look at a thing
so much as within
and through.

You might see it in its element,
in its own light,
and not the lens you would
perceive it through.

See everything unique,
standalone.
And not in sepia
or rose-coloured tints,

but in the ordinary,
the hard edge,
the rounded curves,
the dents.

See a thing as marred
and yet solidly real,
comfortingly soft,
engaging in its honesty.

See the moment as it is,
imperfect,
but quite beautiful enough.
Exquisite even

if understood as infinitesimal,
within the magnitude of moments
in front, behind.

And see this infinitesimal,
finite moment expand.
Expand from gratitude,
expand from focused attention.

And then lift your line of sight
from the books on the shelf,
the bulbs in a jar,
the painting you've now fallen into

and see your lover,
your friend, your child
or house-mate,
your parents, across the room,

and smile,

just a little stunned by the sudden clarity
arising from this small decision
to give your full attention.

RIVERS

It is yours.

I just caught it, pocketed it as a leaf
in a gust of wind,
or a shell among many
at the water's edge.

I just listened for it,
distinguished it
amongst the background noise.
Ringing as all real poetry, clear
as a singing bowl.

Although it is yours,
it is like the river
in which you stand,
not knowing beginning from end,
just that it flows.

And who can say
whether the river is in the water
that is here and gone,
or the topography of land,
the bank and the riverbed underneath.

So it is with this.

This poetry that comes
and lands at will
upon my page,
finds these hands.

But to whom it belongs?

If I kept it,
found a frame to keep it still,
it would lose hold of the life
that underpins it,
would become a stagnant brook.

Instead it finds you,
knows its name upon your tongue,
though neither of us have met before.

And it not only settles in
like all good gifts,
but lives itself out
as the ever-changing thing it is.

And even you find it hard to note
what in an instant can make it yours,
but just as my pen is touched as scribe
you stand willing to be found,

wanting a word to make its home,
and I knee deep in shifting sands
hear the river singing on.

BELONGING

BACKBONE

By our backbones, our fanning ribs,
we mirror the mountains.

The way they lie prone, arched,
with their offshoots of rock,
their gentle foothills.

By our backbones we stretch,
unfurl as a ribbon of mountains
running into the sea.

And sit
by our backbones connected,
to Papatūānuku, our grounding mother.

That with our eyes canvassing the land,
the sky,
we centre into the full circle.

More ancient than the cry of a hawk
across the valley—
this link that brings us back

into the folds of our mother's arms,
our father's gaze—

to close our eyes
and absorb a view,
a history that is part of us,

a remembrance older than the earth.

BELONGING

There is a country to which you belong,
a home that calls you.

More than soil underfoot,
it is a taonga carried in the heart.
A sacred containment of yourself,
a nugget of truth.

And you will know if this home is affirmed
or discredited
in how you feel.

In the grief that sits as a stone
blocking the passageway
to the stream of your dignity,
your true nature.

Or the lightness of spirit
that accompanies validation,
of finding your own clothes
and wearing them.

There is a country unique to any other,
and it does not carry any formal signs
of identification.

But you will know it as a sigh escaping,
of relief,
of the warmth that travels up to own each vessel
of your life's blood now stirred to expression.

And you will sit on the hill overlooking the vista of yourself,
and see how the sun illuminates the fields
of many colours,
all the degrees of shade and light.

And you will expand,
the lightness that is in you
now knowing no bounds,
every ill-fitting garment shreds at your feet,
the fullness of yourself inhabited.

TWO SEAS

In Aotearoa,
at the Northernmost tip,
two seas come to meet,
ragged at the edges,
their waves in full tilt,

pummelling with all
the strength
of twin bodies in
full momentum,
colliding.

In Aotearoa,
at the spindly tip,
there is a lighthouse pointing
due North—
and East, South, West.

Although a lighthouse
doesn't point.

It turns its light, a beacon
circling,
in full view from each
direction.
And does not speak
even,

but is clearly seen
for being bright, high,
constant.

In Aotearoa
the Pacific meets the Tasman
and neither will give way.

Behind them an ocean
of weight,
a predisposition

to spread out
where there is no
hindrance.

But underneath the waves
are currents,
and movements deep
that are older than the
naming of the seas.

And there are fish
and whales,
and sea creatures
for which the seas are an
ecosystem, a wide ocean.

And there are no lines
drawn in sand.
No belonging
to one body of water
over another.

Only blue, green,
and light shining
from above,
and underneath the ocean,
a well of silence.

Somehow like us
when all our angst lays down,
and we remember
how we are tied
by tendrils older
than any reason for parting.

If I speak in the tongues of men or of angels,
but do not have love,
I am only a resounding gong
or a clanging cymbal.

— 1 Corinthians 13:1

MY SONG

This is my song.
My yellow throat
and breast,
my green wing tips.
If I tried to be anything I am not,
I couldn't.
I have no dark coat to shield
this bright sheen.
I have nothing to do
but own my appearance.
And my unique trill of a voice,
ringing high and sweet.
This is my song.
My being outpouring.

And this is us each.
As many species in the world
as communities of people,
as cultures, as personalities.
I rub you one way, and you rub me
so that sometimes we grate,
and at other times,
come together,
a beautiful perfect fit
of yin and yang.

May we never not be
what we are,

while still walking gently.
An ever-blending masterpiece of art.
A sea that gives way
to the tidal river
in its flowing in and out.

See me, my friend,
my lover,
my son, my neighbour.
How I am all yellow coat
and sweet singing voice
to your deep baritone,
and fuller presence.
We can do nothing
but love who we are,
and honour the essence
of one another.

HEART STRINGS

When you wear your heart on your sleeve
you are likely to leave it places.
It will beat and mark every territory as its own.
When you carry your heart in your eyes,
or at the tip of your nerve endings,
it will feel like a fragile thing buffeted
by all the senses.
But it is not so soft.
That you can pick it up
from anywhere it seeks to plant itself.
Brush it off, set it again upon your back,
your front. Know its resilience.
How it is always looking ahead,
whilst still reminding us
in the way it grasps and cleaves,
that nowhere is without a pulse,
a life force ever pregnant with meanings.
God and the ancestors live everywhere
and everywhere is home.

A HOUSE

Build your house.

Build your house high
as branches seeking the light,
build your house wide
as the stretch of ocean,
up-sweep of sky.

Build your house
that every room is occupied,
everyone encompassed,
and anyone who does not have a name
finds their place.

Build your house,
that its ceiling is formed
from mountains meeting,
and its walls from windows
all opening out.

Build your house
out of everything necessary,
and nothing that is of real import
beyond the means
they contribute to love,

to its flowering,
its windfall of blessings,
its riot of blossoming in the spring,
its sweet round apples in fall.

MARRIAGE

We become one another
in this marriage of opposites.
How you may not be me
but you know me,
enough to know what it is
that is me.
And I know you,
to have you, whole, here
near my heart, indwelling
as the sea creature in its shell.
That we accommodate one another,
our differences, our sameness,
in this one bed
in which we move and live.
That we are a bigger being
for being one of two,
a part of the other
who is a part of us.
How we are richer
for the expansion,
the learning of the love
which carves itself a hollow
in which we both fit,
curled and fluid,
moving as we do
in different positions
but bringing the other
with us.

COLONIES

We can sometimes be a colony of seagulls
squabbling over food.

Or tuis, jostling in the air for territory.

A litter of kittens,
mewling blind for milk.

We can be so unkind,
climbing over each other for a teat.

Who is not for me,
someone once said,
is working against.

Which means I think,
among other things,
the house that hurts itself will fall,

a pack of cards without support.

If we have axes to grind,
then let us do them outside,
away from the whare.

Seagulls are seagulls still
flocking in the evening sun.

Tuis will soften their feathers,
and kittens lick each other's coats.

We are too proud I suspect,
thinking ourselves an island
or a mouthpiece.

We might yet eat our many words.
The truth is we live within a village
and we are stronger for the tribe.

A tribe that might be forgiven,
and might forgive each other much
for being subject to one another,

for being made of love.

THE COLOUR OF SKY

Somewhere there is water
the colour of sky.

I know two nights ago my son and I,
in the kitchen sustaining cuts,
were passing words as little paring knives,

when later I watched him
on the deck looking up,
his proud back poised,
his neck a funnel for the pouring sky.

The world then turning
a dusky pink,
in a sunset swathe laid
in each direction.

Where the sun was sinking
we could not see,
just knew we'd been disarmed,
tapped on the shoulders while ruminating.

And somewhere, we each know
there is always water the colour of sky,
always a sun rising
and sinking.

Always a still pool with its surface unbroken,
but for fish and birds.
And we, in our small goldfish bowls
carrying on

as though we had all the reason to.
As though it matters
as to who is right.
When all that matters, is that we pay attention,

watch,
contemplate,
see how as caged birds we fight,
though the door is wide open.

Our territories so large
as to merge as one
between sea and sky.
Somewhere,
here even.

One of the hardest things to make a child understand is,
that down underneath your feet, if you go far enough,
you come to blue sky and stars again;
that there really is no 'down' for the world,
but only in every direction an 'up.'

— Anne Gilchrist

TOGETHER

One thing we each agree on,
the world is in turmoil.

One thing we know
about the other,

we are each of us
deeply troubled.

One thing we share
in common,

universal fear
and confusion,

a need for certainty.

One thing we will have for each other,
numerous opinions.

And one thing this will do,
increase divisions.

Understand everyone is afraid
and will hold on to a piece of wood

if it appears to be floating.

One thing then we must do,
look out for one another.

We are people on a lifeboat
adrift on the sea.

Each of us of more import
than what separates.

No matter, we argue over
what brought us here,

or where now to head.

Have compassion
for your neighbour's needs,

their quavering hearts.

When people are lost at sea
there is a reason they name them souls.

See how love protects,
how hope perceives a horizon.

WEATHER SYSTEMS

We can only make peace within ourselves.
Peace, the living room we reside in,
welcome others,
step forth trailing clouds.

Our literal home, only a series of rooms,
a roof, a floor, windows.
We interact with each other as weather systems
let in from out of doors,

and create the atmosphere
with what we've made important.
That we are siblings, daughters, sons,
life partners,

these are just the facts as they appear,
when the truth is
we are a blizzard that rattles the panes,
or wind that chills the floorboards,

that we need not open doors
for gusts of rain.

And we are both the mainsails
and the breezes that set direction,

the candle on the windowsill
and the person flapping by
shuddering the wallboards,
and wavering its flame.

And we are the fire and its heat,
the essence of rose from candle wax,
or flowers in a vase,
the warmth of a tucked-in blanket over knees.

We cannot underestimate our interactions.
How we choose what to bring
and what to leave
in the holy chamber of another's presence.

We are each other's greatest influencers,
the givers of oxygen
and its removers.
We are the forecasters that set the scene.

In rain and sun,
wind or frost,
or the benign, long length of evening
when peace has won.

Matter is spirit moving slowly enough to be seen.

— Pierre Teilhard de Chardin

ONE FOREST

We are four corners of a quilt.
Four trees in a park, leaves touching.
Not one of us
who walks fast one way,
can leave without an impact on the whole.
The way we are interlinked,
woven together in threads of green and gold,
each bearing another up.

We are each one corner of one another.
No one of us entirely ourselves,
so that when we run
we boomerang back together.
Not enmeshed so much
as mutually reliant,
tied by strands of commitment,
need and love.

How grace must be our main thread.
The connecting binding stitches
which keep us linked.
How shame and guilt are garden vines
that smother—
the wairua of each of us,
a river flowing in our midst.

How we are strong for the
aroha at our hearts.
Our weak links,
the thread another collects
to faithfully unpick,
weave again.

How our quilt is made for warming,
our trees for shade.
How everything that tests us
draws us nearer to the truth,
and everyone who resists
this rub of love, misses out—

on the relief of calm after storm,
the way we look through softened eyes
to see ourselves mirrored
in the other's gaze,
the way we dance
when the winds of the spirit move us
and we sway together in one motion.

Almost forgetting we are two, three, four,
connected as we are at the hips,
the roots.

FOUR SEASONS IN A DAY

It gets better.
If life is a day,
stretched out from hopeful start to end,
then we watch for it to get better.
Sometimes it can seem
that a winter's worth of fronts
roll in before noon.

But if a day is made up
of the four seasons circulating,
then spring is ever turning up.
Sometimes surprising us
in the way defiant blossoms
brace themselves against the wind.

Or jonquils mistake a winter's
false spring, appearing
brave and optimistic,
unfazed by inconsistent weather.

It gets so much better.
And if it doesn't,
we get more practised
at seeing the good.
At panning for it like gold,
sifting through the river's sediment
for something shining.

And when we find it, we run around
exclaiming at our good fortune,
the nugget that weighs little more
than a feather,
enough to dine on for several months.

And the young are looking at us
as though we have lost our heads,
we at the back end of our days
going through our camera rolls.

How can we not
see all the holes in the day—they say.
And we are not seeing valleys
but hillocks for climbing
and perceiving the changing view.

Or we are curling up in bed,
listening to rain on the roof.
Believing in the hope
that life gets ever better.
That nothing remains the same
is the eternal comfort
we each slowly learn.
And we, who have already lived
to half past one,
say to the newbies:

slow down and make coffee
or tea.
Watch the front come in and shake
the blossoms from the cherry tree,
to then go again
just as quickly.

That the new lambs
resume their frolicking,
and the sun its descent
beyond the hill.

THE MIDDLE

It is hard in the middle.

The middle is the fresh pain in our limbs
after the climb.

The middle is the plateau
where we thought we would see the view,

the end rising up,
a tantalising beacon,

but instead, see the trees
on the next rise.

It is hard in the middle
to see how far we've come.

And if we do,

it seems too much a stretch
to contemplate its doubling.

Not when our thirst is a rasp in the throat
and our lungs pushed to bursting,

our hunger a gnawing edge.

Yes, it's hard in the middle
before our second wind.

Our faith and hope now crumbs
in our backpacks.

We, at the point of turning
where there's no way back.

That hard realisation from which grows resilience.

Ah, it's hard in the middle,
so we sit and take stock.

Draw together as people around a fire
keeping warm.

'What do we still have?'
becomes the question on our tongues.

'And what can we make of it?' the answer,
like a lantern shedding light.

It is hard in the middle,

but sometimes what we need
is not a given at the beginning,

but developed like a muscle in the walking.

Or we must wait for it
as pilgrims charting stars,

that the conditions themselves
might become an opening.

YOUR HEART

Take your heart, a torch to the field,
and watch it catch the dry foliage alight,
set it all aflame.

And know your heart
as a light that is not easily diffused,
or constrained.

But as a source of endless vitality
in how it revives itself.
How its grace

is always an invitation
to another being,
to assure themselves of worth, regardless.

Regardless of their broken state,
their right/left feet,
their limitations.

Or it's a peace flag, in how it initiates a truce
leading to understanding,
redemption.

Take your heart, a flame to a field,
always more tinder dry that it appears,
and watch it take.

How its light is like the sun,
or the stars,
just needing an impetus to start
a reaction at the core,

to then emanate out
a glowing beacon.

And by this fire
warm yourself,
know how you made it all yourself.

And see how like love
in its incandescent fervour,
it radiates,

how your neighbour's face is
now all alight,
their own heart burning bright.

We do not truly see light,
we only see slower things lit by it.

— C.S. Lewis

PILGRIMS

'Start how I mean to go on...',
one friend said.

Yes, all that deters us are the elements,
the upwards slopes, the rocky terrain.
But we have each other.

We just need one or two to begin
and we can follow their tracks.
Find behind them the landmarks.

We might even hear them call back,
'Don't miss this view',
or 'the wildflowers are blooming'.

Yes, if we are quiet and observant
on our walk,
we might find even the landscape speaks.

A beauty we might miss
if we had stayed in place.

So look, look now for the ones walking out,
provisioned,
chins up.

Trust their faith filled, courageous stance,
their positive declarations.
And come in behind.

These the God anointed trackers,
the map makers.
We the pilgrims needing friends,

holding hands.
Bringing with us the weak
and the tired.

We all have our own journeys,
no route quite the same
for what we see, experience.

But, the starters, they are our lanterns
and our compasses,
our map-makers.

Follow them.

STARS

Here I am closer to the stars.
As the night grows dark the stars draw nearer.

Just as today, when I looked in water so clear
as to see beneath,

the stars hang in a translucent sky
that its depths displayed are an open book.

Today I am higher to be near the stars,
the beat of bird wing, the forest night calls.

And the sky is a blanket under which we live,
not unnoticed, unaccountably blessed.

And now that the moon has shook her golden mane,
all the lingering clouds have flown,

and all that exists is a high dark dome,
studded as a city of lights.

That each star has travelled so many light years
to find me here alone and alive –

that some have died and long expired
before their light arrives in my sight –

is a wonder I cannot easily fathom,
while sitting here touched by its very truth.

THIS CLOSE

More central than gravity
I pivot on you,
as on the eye of the needle.

More present than air
I walk in you,
as the sea surrounding.

My eyes cannot focus
on the things too near,
but you still live here,

just a hair's breadth away.

And I swing, as the planets
in their circle,
hardly knowing the force that pulls.

But feeling nonetheless
an inkling,
as breath on skin,

or a cool breeze,
bringing goose-bumps
in its wake.

Yes, we each live
more central to you
than we understand.

Like a people
in proximity
to creatures beyond count,

who hardly know
they're not alone.

And on your pivoting
planet,
are courted

by you,
who have burst the seams of intimacy
to touch us from inside out.

FURTHER

It is right now
when the world feels stopped on its axis,

that we need the things that continue,
remain the same.

It is now, when a week feels a month,
and a year, too far,

that we need the furthest things.

The sky and the stars,
the thought of the galaxies.

The night canvas that has looked the same
across aeons.

To know
that private and common griefs
and every shade of ecstasy

remain unchanged at a distance,
and across centuries.

That we see the same moon
as the remembered saints,

and those who loved
and died unknown to history,

this is now our immeasurable comfort.

That we might be one with them,
who breathed and struggled

and trusted in patience,
in a world stopped at a tilt precarious.

Yes, it is now, when a week feels a month
and a year too far,

that we need the furthest things.

The sky and the stars,
the thought of the galaxies.

This night's vastness,
the same across aeons.

Let nothing trouble you.
Let nothing scare you.
All is fleeting. God alone is unchanging.
Patience everything obtains.
Who possesses God
nothing wants.
God alone suffices.

— St Teresa of Avila

WEATHER FORECAST

Today I will remember my grounded-ness
in the rising winds.
Not resist it.

Nothing has changed.
I am still here planted
near the river in the green world.

Today here, I will remember I am like the tree,
its up-reach of branches,
cascade of leaves.

That no matter the direction of the breeze,
the wind's strength,
or the storm's deluge,

I, who have lived now fifty years,
no less I suspect than the Liquid Amber
out my windows,

am planted.

And when I find it hard to muster strength,
enthusiasm for the year ahead,
a future of unknowns,

I think of the tree's sap, running to the tips of limbs,
its towering trunk,
how there is no question of it ceasing production.

How the tree's many leaves,
carried on all the vicissitudes of the winds,
need the guarantee of life to flow.

Which, if I look back
it has for me,
for all,

despite the seasons,
the weather systems,
the forecast winds.

BEAUTY TO SURVIVE

We need beauty to survive,
that we drink her in mouthfuls.

Rising up out of the mist,
resilient as the sun.

Not one day does she say—

today I will lie in,

as today the world
does not need me.

No, her duty of making beauty
the sacred art it is

is her life's work,
spanning millennia.

She, so centered on each of us,

as though she were our personal
attendant,

our undeserved returning
blessing.

The Divine Voiceless One,
who speaks her ancient blessing

on all of us who cross her path.

Who, living by the name of God,
gives us all

reason for being.

DAYLIGHT

Watch the shadows flee in the morning,
chased by a million sun rays.

What can compete against the light
and its great eraser,

casting her wide luminous net,

sending into oblivion
the dark and its minions.

Yes, who can stand up to the light?
Stare her in the eye?

So when fear breaks itself like a sea
upon your chest,

sore
but still breathing,

then open your eyes
and see the light dawning.

Watch how she enters,
great empress,

shooing the crowd from the temple.

Or casts, like a fisherman,
her net,

the sea for a moment
broken.

INGRAINED

When God made the world
with his curved hand
as a potter at the wheel,

he found he could not
willingly separate
from his design.

In the midst of creating,
he foresaw how he might remain,
ingrain himself

as ink upon skin,
glaze upon clay,
as a river with its blue vein,

threaded through the green.

And so, God peopled the earth
as a painter dabbing colours,
building light upon a canvas.

And finding it was good—
this stretch of world with
its blanket of foliage, circle of blue—
declared that it was finished.

This work of creation,
through which he himself existed,
so carefully embedded
as the stars in the heavens.

TANGLES

What's the pattern?
All we see are tangles.
Like the maze of childhood with hedges
veering skywards
as though Heaven held the key.
Or like the games of snakes and ladders,
that slippery slide
that seemed to be up to a flick of the wrist,
or a lay of dice.
As though some people had all the luck,
come by easy,
carried in the genes.

What's the pattern?
I'm less inclined to think Heaven
is a source of answers,
a hoard of carefully tied up ends.
I think instead
that seeing the back of everything
is less about discerning meaning,
than learning to leave what's been behind.
To see the currents flowing
and spinning,
and flung from a whirlpool
carry on,
surveying a new evolving scene.

What's the pattern?
If it's random,
then in some ways that
is freeing,
meaning dead ends are not
inevitable outcomes.
And if it's orchestrated,
then why not believe
in the divine inspiration of a mind
beyond our perceiving.
Why not abide in the peace of trusting,
than strain the mind to understand.

What's the pattern?
How different it is
from where we're sitting.
To the fish in the sea, to the bird in the sky,
a reef is a length of rocky island,
or a deep-water home of hills and caverns.
What is the meaning?
Take the moment as a length of string,
threaded and twirled through
long boned fingers,
watch it fall in a myriad of patterns.
Or take your grandmother's crocheted rug
and turn it over to view the stitches,
see how the intricate woven designs
cause the flowering blooms to flourish.

The feeling remains that God is on the journey, too.

— St Teresa of Avila

HOOKED

I see the trees pointing up
as guideposts.
I see the grass as a coverage,
a blanket for the world.
I see the way the green unfurls
across the earth
and think of my daughter's
crocheted scarf
lengthening under love's firm labours,
its hours of soothing repetition.

I turn now in a widening circle.
My house a centrepiece
among the clouds,
a lamp light mirroring sunset hues,
now gold, now apricot,
now indigo blue.
I see the way night's curtain
folds,
as a swaddling cloth
or an encompassing hand.

And I see the way I live pointing up,
guided by above, beneath.
I see the way my surrounds speak
in a myriad of languages,
the only constant, this signature
running unrestrained

through all things,
alive in the veins
of each limb and leaf,
each bird's span of wing.

This is the religion I profess,
though I have no guidance to provide
in following it.
Other than to say: Look.
See how you are like a crocheted pattern,
a finished loop attached
to the one following it.
Expanding outwards, lengthways.
Know that you are in line for continuance,
so very gently hooked
and interlocked.

EARTHY GRACE

Grace is somewhat like the earth.
How she waits like a mother,
her wide lap
a place we play, are soothed,
held at the breast.

The earth is like that,
all grace in the face of what we do to her.
How given just enough of rain or sun,
she will still do her best to blossom,
though we might tax her resources,
scramble over governorship.

So comes grace,
like the sun in her regal state,
rising and turning the other cheek
in her traversing of the sky.

Grace of the earth,
of the elements.
Those who deny knowledge of God
have not thought of the sun
and the rain as a benediction.

Have not understood how grace comes
unbidden, and not differentiating
between deserving or not—
does not even ask the question.

How the mother with the wide lap
has bought and wrapped her presents
for the birthday child.
She is not counting misdeeds.
So we are graced by the earth,
loved by its creator,
no matter our indifference.

As though the world were a garden
made for us,
and a way of demonstrating without words
what love looks like unmasked.
Patient, gracious, long suffering.

Every day appearing arms wide open
and beautiful as the pure face of God.
Beauty in the end,
the key that opens the heart's door,

draws us to care and to register
the gifts strewn at our feet,
the breathing, humming mother love
of God's heart for us.

GOD KICKS

Mary felt God kick under her ribs.
I imagine sometimes she laid down at night
and felt a foot against
the walls of her womb,
and would try to trace it along her wide abdomen,
would take Joseph's hand
and place it on top of the groundswell of movement,
wait for his gaze to meet hers.

And Mary felt God clasp down upon her breast
with his hungry mouth,
lips working to draw milk,
his small fists against her pliant flesh.
And I imagine she thought about watering
the source of life,
the wonder of that,
how everything turns in circles.

And Mary felt God's small hand in her own palm,
his fingers in her hair,
and his soft lips on her cheeks.
That perhaps Joseph looked at the Mother of God
to realise then
there existed no woman more blessed,
in the short years of infancy,
where to an infant
there is no sense of separation, or distance,
between mother and child.

Yes, I think Joseph must have looked at Mary with awe,
she being the bearer of light into the world
and the sustainer of it.
That every woman following Mary
retains the mystery still
surrounding birth,
and can close her eyes,
feel God at her breast.

And I think God too, remembers.
The way he talks about his body,
a people made up of parts
belonging to each other,
the sacredness of all the different
elements,
bound together in unity.

I know one day I thought of a little girl,
and then suddenly there she was walking.
What if God is a thought to which we give birth,
and we, the mysterious conduits?
I know, even though I no longer have a womb,
I can feel God hidden under my ribs.

THE WORD

Nameless you come slipping
out of the eternity,
and nameless you sink yourself
a stone in the pond of our being.

That nameless we come to know you
and to call you beloved.
And known, we come to call ourselves
beloved.

YHWH, the name above all names,
who comes with all the secrets of the universe
ingrained,
implants himself

that we know ourselves,
not by an echo of a sound
or breath,
but by the very Word of Life itself.

That we see ourselves
in the face of the one who,
though undefinable,
is named in every language.

Though definitions
can't match the Word
from which the world was sown as seed
to become the green continuum it is.

YHWH,
you come alongside us with soundless feet
to bring to awareness
our sacred selves beheld in you.

And named we learn
to call ourselves beloved,
and to call you by the name
love gives our tongue—

Emmanuel,
God with us.

HOLY LOVE

When God makes love to you
there are no defences.
Holy love, so purifying
as to wring us out.
Hang us to dry.

When God chases after you
there is no hiding around corners.
There is only, 'Come get me!'
Waiting for the light to
flush us out.

When God takes hold of you
there is no resistance.
Only hands
reaching upwards in response.

So that your grip on God
has him now weak-kneed
and responsive.
His love for you
a cymbal ringing out.

A planet in the propelling
force of turning,
a river in the way
it builds up to a flood.

When God makes love to you
you are on the summit of the world.
God showing you with his mirror
the beauty of your face,

that ultimately you then
see yourself in everyone,
and everyone irrevocably beloved.

SYMBIOSIS

At your feet are the roots of all.
Do you see yourself an island,
a sole separate being?
How deceived are we
by appearances?

At your back is the weight of generations.
At your feet, an interlinked web of communication.
In the air, chemicals that speak.
So much in nature
we are learning to understand,
shall never fully comprehend.

One thing we know,
with our atoms made of stardust,
our breath, a collaboration with the trees,
is that each of us here
is in intimate participation
with the systems
of which we're a thread.

One thing we know, the world
has made a way for us
that in humility we might hold
out our hands.
Survival of the fittest
meaning less about dominion
than a willingness to cooperate,

bowing at the same time
we stand.

When I come near the red peony flower
I tremble as water does near thunder,
As the well does when the plates of earth move,
or the tree when fifty birds leave at once.

— From 'At the Time of Peony Blossoming' by Robert Bly

ISLANDS

I spy an island
far across a chasm of waves and sea.

I spy an island
not so different to me perhaps,

except for the space that separates.

I spy an island
that I must guess at its flora and its fauna.

Not holding binoculars,

only holding in my hands
the total sum of my experience—

if that even,

so dependent is everything
upon our understanding of it.

I spy an island,
closer if I close my eyes,

connected underneath as we are
by bridges of rock and substrate,

and sharing as we do an ocean full
of H2O and sea salts,

a myriad of organisms.

That it does not matter really,
if this other isle is made of pines

and I am covered in brush and tea tree.
Not when underneath

we are joined somewhere
at the ligaments,

in the muscle and bone of the ground.

Yes, I spy an island
and calling close my eyes,

that the birds might travel to and fro
from us each,

alighting upon leaves,
and the same sea move itself,

a giant body of weight between us
two islands,

not so small after all,
when you consider the whole.

ISLANDS

BEYOND

I can see a garden,
and beyond that a lake,
and beyond that a mountain,
and beyond that the sky.

Everything lying beyond,
so that we must travel beyond
each layer of perception
to find the central sphere.

And even that
when reached,

is a garden
with a lake behind,
and behind that a mountain,
and behind that

the wide, enveloping sky.

ALONE

God gives us a strange autonomy,
two legs and arms, a heart and mouth,
one mind.

A room sometimes of our own.
A silent house. A life contained.
An ache for a ghostlike limb.

That nature is both interlinked
and impartial.
Wired for this greater work
of surviving,

to leave us in a sense,
alone.

Intimately connected,
while aware of each limit of our influence,

each prayer into the wind,
and bounding echo in the void,
each shedding of ourselves.

How without us
the world will turn,

        that we,

    a land cut off from the main,
    will feel ourselves an island.

Or a tree above the undergrowth,
    growing in maturity,
    learning what can't be held.

Yes, that God gives us a strange autonomy,
    a prelude for letting go,
    a sense that all our control

    must like the body give up,
        give in,
    is the strange secret of growth.

    We, in our understanding,
    learn how little we own.
    We, in our imagined success,

    learn to leave behind
everything loved and borrowed.
All we've sought to call 'mine.'

DIGNITY

Perhaps standing up for ourselves
is more making a space around ourselves.

One in which we move
as a water drop undisturbed.

A drop, that is part of the ocean,
or the stream, or a shower,
but is also contained

and is entirely water on its own terms.

Perhaps moving through the world
with courage and dignity
is knowing what we hold inside,

around, as a field of wildflowers,
as mountains, streams and oceans,

with everyone asking to swim in us,
or pick our blooms,
first needing permission.

Yes, to have a door we can shut while moving
is our birth-right,
ours and everyone living,

so that we might move together in a shelter
made of this knowledge of our worth,

with keys to our own precious kingdoms,
and self-respect our doorman,

and a space of at least an arm's length
in which we swim throughout the world.

CONCESSIONS

I recognise you—
we say to the ache that makes itself known.

Though each day you wear a different disguise
you still feel the same.

You settle into the same thin space
between our rib bones and our hearts.

Where you remind the arms of their powerlessness to hold anything.
The heart of its incapacity for control.

And when we hear of a friend's sudden grief,
we ask you, ache, to make room,

that we might come alongside you,
take your hand and hers,

feel the common bond of unity
sorrow invokes,

the empathy that loss carves in us each
to make a larger space for love.

Yes, I recognise you, my frequent guest.
How you arrive so quietly

that it's not until I feel the knot tight in my chest,
the fruitless flutter of my hands,

that I know you come again
with the eternal question,

'What will I concede to you today?'

A LEAF

In the universe there is a small leaf floating.

It might seem alone
amongst the myriad of stars,
the dark expanse, the circling solar winds.

But on the leaf's surface is a small world floating.
Miniscule and intricate,
a little universe in a nutshell.

And in this minute universe
there are countless forests leading back,
path upon path into eternity.

And many more leaves than there are trees.
And each leaf afloat
upon the autumn gusts,

a singular world enclosed,
and encircled too by solar winds
and planets,

and stars bright as pin pricks,
luminous
in the darkness.

Yes, in this universe within a universe,
within a revolving eternity,
there is a small leaf floating,

and not as alone as it seems—

the dark night,
a deep bassinet,
the solar winds,
its gentle rocking—

as the Holy One
moving across waters,

and carrying us each,
light as we are,

feathers upon God's breath.

ENCIRCLED

God catches me looking through windows,
opening windows.

He catches me walking up hills, past doors,
tripping myself up in ribbons.

He sees me shifting deadwood.

And he watches me, lost in a forest,
forgetting the seasons.

God, my confidante,
my absolution,

watches me looking through windows.
Gives me reason as my stable anchor.

Reminds me how the river ever flows
in one direction.

How the seasons change,
not in retrospect,

but sometimes when
we've not readied ourselves.

And God, catching me looking
through windows,

is the drawer of blinds,
is the locksmith, the hill leveller,

the gardener,
the shepherd.

God sees me
throwing stones for attention,

or lost forgotten in a forest,
guessing the season.

And circling over me
in a great cloud of golden leaves,
a sea of barren limbs,

a cluster of green tipped branches,
an avalanche of blossom.

The place where you are right now
God circled on a map for you.
Wherever your eyes and arms and heart can move
against the earth and the sky,
the beloved has bowed there-
The beloved has bowed there knowing
You were coming...

— Hafiz

HEART QUAKE

I am a bird, who has drawn its cage around.
A spinning top,
which has spun itself into delirium.
A body, cushioned by the ocean,
sinking into oblivion.

That the head leads
right up until the heart quakes and stops,
is a truth we are forced into accepting.

How when I rise I am an eagle,
and when, through weariness or grief,
or fear, I descend,
I am a stone gathering speed
before coming to a sudden jolting halt.

Or I am a crescent moon low
on the horizon,
receding as a tide at its ebb,
to then gather momentum to turn
and come flooding as moonlight on a field.

OVERCOMING

The one who has already overcome
sends us messages from the homeland.

In little scraps of leaf, decaying.
In the sun's endless rising,
in the quiet of the woodland
before the world's dawn.

When I am alone
I see myself already overcome,
fast forwarded,

or rather stepped into the eternity
that I also live within.

My re-entry to the world and its demands
is like a role I'm given,
but never as true
as my vocation to draw apart.

Each of us has this vocation,
the way the Divine enters in
to remind us who we are,
drawing us into the cosmos to dance.

Never let that go.
Never forget you are both eternal
and deeply present in the flow of life,
a river without beginning or end.

That we can step out from ourselves
is the gift we are given,
the very means of our overcoming
amidst the day's obligations.

Every now and then live
for love of yourself
in relationship with life.

It is a refueler,
this reminder why we are born.

I am the fiery life of the essence of God;
I am the flame above the beauty in the fields;
I shine in the waters; I burn in the sun, the moon, and the stars.
And with the airy wind, I quicken all things
vitally by an unseen, all-sustaining life.

— Hildegard of Bingen

GILT EDGED

The cloud had her gilt edges
all lit by sun.

These shimmery thin tendrils
through which the light shone.

While the rest of her, subdued
in modest grey,

even if she sought to,
would not have drawn the eye.

Not in the same way
as her edges,

all soaring and silver rimmed,
all insubstantial and sheer as muslin,

set adrift in the evening sky.

How today, I still think of her,
one day on—

in the way an artist might
who did not have his camera or a brush,

but can recall
at the closing of his eyes

each shape forming
her substance,

each measure of light.

Or, a philosopher perhaps,
who drives a way further on

and thinks to himself
of Rumi,

how the light enters directly
through the wound.

How it's at the edges
where we are our most frail,

most vulnerable,
that the Beloved finds an entry point.

And our own beauty, an outlet.

I said: what about my eyes?
He said: Keep them on the road.

I said: What about my passion?
He said: Keep it burning.

I said: What about my heart?
He said: Tell me what you hold inside it?

I said: Pain and sorrow.
He said: Stay with it.
The wound is the place where the Light enters you.

— Rumi

NEVER ENDING

Hold on to the leaf turning,
it will show you how to die.

Note it's change through the hues
from green to orange to yellow.
Then watch it give itself up to brown,
before the free-fall.

Hold on.

Feel yourself a forgotten universe.
This is the one instant you will remember flight.

It coming back to you afresh,
as the moment before
you first came to consciousness,
when there was no need of memory.

Then lay down
with the tree a shelter above you.

Now is the time for the earth to yield
its secrets,
the Great Mother's fertile expanse
a rich bed to enfold you.

That dying now
becomes a coming home.

A new awareness of the whole
and your sacred role within it.

Hold on.

Can you feel the warmth below, above?

The earth is drawing nearer to the sun
and the days are lengthening.
There are stirrings in the earth.

The seeds are burgeoning
in preparation for their burst into
eager sprouts of green.

Look up.

See how the tips of branches are
topped with leaf bud.

Before you wish yourself amongst them
at their tender beginnings,
remember how your green leaf
decaying,
has helped give them a carpet
from which to draw sustenance.

In this great circle
the whole is always alive.
And death is recalled again
as the great misconception it is.

And life remembered as the
cycle never ending.

AROUND THE SUN

Around the sun in 365 days
goes the world.
Not a falter in her flight
she orbits in the clutch of gravity.

And round we go,
unaware of how seasons are ordained,
or perhaps more,
are a fact of nature's momentum.

Round we go,
and when I reflect back, I see
how I've spiralled
from life's first breath
to now.

Sometimes spun
as a spinning top,
disoriented, uncomprehending.

Sometimes as a dancer,
pirouetting,
within the flow of graceful strength.

And sometimes
as a leaf suspended,
at the mercy of the untamed winds.

I do best then
to hold things lightly
as the world is carried,

sustained by ancient laws
of perpetuation
for millennia.

I do best when I do not resist
the change of season,
the continuity of movement,
the finality of yesterday.

I do best to stay on board,
expectant,
seeing how in the flow
my central core remains unchanged.

Just like gravity,
our protector from dissolution
and the enabler of our passage,

keeps us poised
and turning.

And so, at the core of things
I trust the Alpha
and Omega,
the cyclical beginnings and endings,

as a genus of seed ever replicating,
bursting, shedding,
spreading,

and above all,
continuing, season by season.

MEMORY OF LIGHT

Sometimes we wonder why the rain,
the winter wind, and falling
ink-black night that sweeps away the light
with heavy curtains.

We wonder why the pain,
how sudden joy can fly,
and grief set in
as frost covers grass, or as ice sets a seal
upon window panes.

How to thaw, with the memory of light
now an uncertain thing,
and hope even,
a story we once told ourselves,
which the dark seeks to steal with the sun.

Yes, we wonder why winter,
barren wilderness,
is at all considered necessary.
How of all our human conditions,
pain and suffering
must make itself so strongly felt.

Like the winter wind
and her inhospitable season
charging in without asking admittance,
hollowing us out
so even our bones sing in a long lament.

A strange song of shock and betrayal,
or a hymn to the remembrance of things,
that in replaying we might postpone
this reduction to winter's bare branches,

her frozen ground and scarce provisions.
Her snatching of joy as a winged bird,
singing out its days to find no breath remaining.

Yes, pain is a cruel trick for love's devotion.
Perhaps love has her seasons, as a woman her children.
Everything is a lesson in letting go.
And even spring is a mirage of the imagination,

until in stubborn grace the shoot
of hope pushes through.

UNKNOWN

Ah God, the Great Unknown.

The closer we perceive you
the further you recede.
The Unknown that can't be expressed,
except through our constructs.
It is better that you remain unknown,
that you can be all we each imagine you to be,
and the answer to our intimate longings.

For what Creator God
has not imagination to express us
and to contain all our expressions.
And wildness to encompass our wildernesses.

Yes, that you allow us to love you as we are
in the private cell of our hearts.
As the silent friend who listens
and holds up a mirror,
so that when we are looking for you
we see ourselves.

God, we are grateful.

That while we feel our way toward you,
and in the dark of our vision might despair,
you are behind us and tapping us gently
as a friend upon the shoulder.

WIND TUNES

You and the day.
Always arriving at one another.
Always an alchemy of sorts.
What the day has in store,
how you meet it
prepared or not.

Waking with your old aches,
your fresh hurts.
Feeling your way in,
each limb a weight tested.
Each stretch a hopeful reach.

How this day does not need to be told
where you're at.
How it's already acutely aware
of what you have to bring to it.
How it will make one hundred allowances
for everything you cannot do.

How the day is not just a blank canvas,
indifferent,
but a welcome mat,
a creative and encouraging accomplice.
Even the painful or unexpected,
anointed in some way
with the beautiful.

So that at the end of your days
you might be able to talk out loud
in everyone's hearing of healing,
how though you shall die
you shall live.

How you have lived up to now,
both broken and whole,
full and empty,
a chamber of possibilities.
Bringing everything forward
for the world to use.

And how she has blown through you,
gauging the sounds
of her breath through your being.
Making of you a wind instrument
that rings true.

The very holes of which you despaired
become now the means for music,
for wind tunes between you and creation.

LIFE IS A POEM

Life is like a poem.
The poem that starts somewhere in the middle
and finishes before the end.
The poem that asks questions
rather than gives answers.
The poem that picks up the thread
someone else started,
and drops it again
before anything can be tied into bows.
And the real poem.
The one to which you paid attention
because it said something resonant
that matched your unspoken thoughts.
Nudged your world a little.

Your life is a poem.
One you can't read as others do.
Your name means something
and your actions together make a story.
It won't be so much the words you say,
as the way they come together on the page
and express something beyond you,
that others will remember.
You, one of many poems in a long continual word
since the creation of the world.
When your pen falls to the page
someone else will collect it up,
and write their name,
and that will be okay.

Okay, that she will say what you thought.
That another will remember and rephrase,
for their children to expand upon.
Everything important has been said,
but not all the ways of saying it.
And that's the thing about creation.
The surprises. And the common threads.
That is why we're not afraid of death.
For what is finished?
Does a poem ever end?
No, every poet knows they could select a thousand endings
with none bringing full resolution.
A poem is a page ever unfolding,
with meanings that change upon the reading.
And like a poem, your life has its definitive voice,
one that is echoing even as you're leaving.

SIDES

Two sides of the coin.

Sorrow and joy,
love and loss.

And the river runs swift.

These life courses
we have placed our faith in.

We can hold them tight in our wallets,

our coins,
the only imprints upon them,

our own hands squeezing,

counting out
our precious acquisitions.

Or we can hold them loosely,

so that they fly
and flip in the wind,

land in the river,

tossed and blown about
by tide and weather.

Circumstance,

or some trick of fate that sees them

now heads, now tails,
joy and pain.

There is a word called serendipity,

which sounds something like
happiness right on cue.

And mischance,

speaking benignly of fortune lost
in a sad, swift stroke

that the gods appear angry.

And then there is calamity,
which echoes in its length

as lament does,
loud,

and then hauntingly soundless.

But better I think
are our wringing hands in the river

than tightly gripped.

This river being more life to some,
more reassuring

and sustaining,

than all the good luck
and fortuitous circumstances

in the world combined.

More of worth than all the coin,
and all the love

we each can possess.

That we are a river,
in which we don't walk but swim in,

is a memory we are to let return,

if we are to live
and laugh even,

with joy and pain engraved,

in inclement weather
and rushing tides.

Aware how

no coin is truly ours,
and without this rushing body

there is no blessing at all,

everything dependent as it is
on the tumultuous whole.

TRAVELLERS

Do you have a light, I hear myself say,
it is dark out.
And a map?
You must know where you're going?
How will you find your way back?
The desert is a great big place,
I'm afraid you'll lose your soul.

How hard it is not to tread the paths
our beloved one's walk?
To test it out first.
How we know these ways are not ours,
and if we walked them
they would take us someplace else.

The road after all,
the makings of both traveller and landscape.
This alchemy of sorts,
where one changes the other
to shape the way forward.

Do you have a faith to follow,
to lean on?
Where is your guidebook?
And your pack of resources?
You are travelling, after all, so light,
how will you be equipped?

'Hush', we are told.
How the one travelling must move far enough
to see themselves alone, both in light and dark,
to pit themselves against the mountain,
to scale it,
to perceive it for the dust it was.

How the desert
is an opening to an inner world,
untouched,
with its hills and vales,
its shadows and its caverns,
its great wide expanses where the wind blows.

How full of hidden streams
and untapped treasures.
How one does not go in
with paraphernalia to keep,
or even faith assured,
but comes out changed,
denuded of scaffolding.

And with something now rooted in him
as a tree, with new leaves.
How he is then able to blossom,
and to fruit.
How, upon hearing the call and responding,
he has met himself and wrestled,
so that any faith emerging is built on truths,

and any consolations received
have been for his true needs,
now unburdened on the mountain's back
and absorbing the sun.

Dare to declare who you are.
It is not far from the shores of silence to the boundaries of speech.
The path is not long, but the way is deep.
You must not only walk there, you must be prepared to leap.

— Hildegard of Bingen

RECALLING ETERNITY

A friend recalled to me today
that we have all of eternity.
There is a scripture verse too

that speaks of our life
as like the grass
that is here today and gone tomorrow.

Sometimes I think
it's a matter of perspective.

For a short while
the roses I picked
from the roadway's wild hedge
seemed to relentlessly bloom,
and then,

at the touch of too much sun,
gave up,
dropped their bold bright heads,
shrivelled to a dusky papery pink.

We may have eternity, yes.
And time both contracts and stretches,
that we might look back,
to find the significant moments, a blur.

Only expansive in the memory
and even then,
embellished to fill the blanks.

Perhaps I'm saying,
we would do well to remember
that time runs fast, rapid
as a mountain burn in spring
after snowmelt.

Everything so seemingly substantial
flowing out over stone,
soaking into the ground.

And yet,
I can't throw my flowers out,
though by all appearances they've died.

They were dead the moment they were cut.
Though they shone bright for a while longer,
and in such a last hurrah that it
makes me wonder

if the moment of our birth
is simply a forgetting,
and death,
a recollection.

And eternity?

Maybe we find eternity is a discovery
of what mattered,
and why.

How perhaps all of it—
the boredom and the angst,
and the ecstasy

were perfect in their brevity,
just like the roses now
given out.

Oh, heart, if one should say to you that the soul perishes like the body, answer that the flower withers, but the seed remains.

— Kahlil Gibran

IMAGINING

I see the trees,
I close my eyes and know somehow
the trees remain.

At the opening of my lids
they will not have moved—

cannot move.

And only I,
in the opening and closing of my eyes,
lose sight of them.

I see the trees,
I close my eyes as darkness falls
and know the trees stand still.

In the opening of my lids
they won't have moved.

Though all I see now
is my own reflection in the window,
the trees in the morning will re-emerge

as something out of the imagination
taken shape.

And I think of the Divine,
how in the night I know the trees
by the sound of the wind in the branches.

And it is not a stretch to think
that God is a memory in the mind
placed there before we were born.

And we sitting here, imagining now
what we can't remember seeing,

just like our eyes in the natural world,
curtailed by the limits of our vision,
know there is more existing.

Like these trees, which after seeing now,
I close my eyes,
dream.

At that hour when all things have repose,
O lonely watcher of the skies,
Do you hear the night wind and the sighs
Of harps playing unto Love to unclose
The pale gates of sunrise?

— From 'At that Hour' by James Joyce

BLOOMING

The blooms of my Michaellia Yunanensis
are falling,
picked up by the winds,
thrown as confetti.
They make a picture on the ground
as much as on the stem.
Nevertheless,
they do not last for long,
either stem-adhered or windborne.
Curling brown at the edge
upon the deck,
or crushed upon the driveway,
embossed with the patterns of tyres.

My Michaellia Yunanensis is a drawcard
for the bees, the butterflies,
and my eyes, as I sit here
in the intermittent spring sunshine.
That their petals are both
intrinsically fragile and tough,
is a life lesson, I think.
How we are brief-lived
in the scheme of things,
with what matters most being
not longevity,
as the measure
of our blooming,
the grace we carry by

raising an open face
to the sun and wind,
whatever may come.

Allowing, as Rilke says,
everything to happen to us—
both beauty and terror.
It's not so terrible perhaps
for the petal who lifted and landed.
Not so terrible,
and very beautiful,
to be one of many
blooming in the spotlight,
fading out,
feeling upon us a weighty impression,
not knowing its pattern.

Disintegrating and
looking up,
seeing in the light
and the haze of white,
a wider purpose.
How we are not just petal,
or leaf, or bloom even,
but tree,
with all its appointed seasons.

HANDS FREE

The only thing you can ever hold
is wonder,
and even then, loosely.
The substance of a thing gets in its way,
the disguise of the whole.
Who of us can see past the solidity of matter,
of shape, that reveals a thing
and hides it too.

And the only way you can ever hold a thing
is loosely. Hands off even
is how you might best see it.
Coming up on quiet trapeze feet,
ready to jump, counter your balance.
Perceive from the corner of your eye
before it shape-changes out of sight.

The only means you will ever see a thing
is with imagination,
in imagining the possibilities.
Perhaps the realest thing about us each
is what we might be if someone
were to envision it.
Like this poem which you might
deaden with attempts to understand.

How does the sky speak to you?
You hold enough knowledge of it
to rest upon a pinhead,
and it speaks because you hardly know it,
all attempts to understand
falling at its feet.
While in your unknowing
you might find yourself a home
in the enveloping dark.

I almost lost the essence of this poem
by making it readable.
Wonder is that thing
that has us coming back for more.
That makes us imagine ourselves
as deeper than our perception.
To imagine ourselves akin
with the things that move and elude us.

To make us imagine the world,
and beauty, love and virtue,
as pinnacles to be reached for.
As possibilities, even more
impossibly radiant
than they are.

WITHIN

There is much
I do not know.

But what I do
is always sufficient.

This awareness
of love.

That we are held in love.

Nothing outside of it,
everything within it.

Love's generosity,
our gift of life.

This life,
a dewdrop on a leaf,

our being
and our continuance

held within an ever-evolving
creation.

For as long as there is love
there is life.

For as long as there is life
we are held in love.

Our separation,
only illusion,

which in Love's grace
we are given to understand.

How we are a word
within the eternal Word

before the world's birth,

and will remain a word
within the Word

never-ending.

Everything up to us,
falling,

and fading out as the world.

Everything outside of Love,
simply the ego
that calls our name,

offering us clothes.

Tempting us with visibility,
insubstantial as the wind.

When we have always been
visible to Love,

and hidden in Love's hand,
always known.

And that we will remain
in love,

is now all we have come
to understand.

This identity,
which was ours
before birth,

after death.

TIME TOMORROW

There is time tomorrow
for everything,
but for poetry
there is only
now,

beckoning
in the way a bubble
builds,
is blown into the wind,
bursts.

There is time for everything
tomorrow,

but the poem
is a piece of driftwood,
sea-glass,
a heart shaped stone,

a small miracle
in the sand
we walk past,
miss,
if not looking.

Though the poem
is a bubble blown,

it's more than
the elements of which
it's comprised.

Connected to its source,
it is the fountain pen
that won't run dry—

or paint,
in the hands of an artist
who lets the canvas
choose the colours,
then follows suit.

How the poet
captures the flow
in the moment lived,
so deft and quick,

adept at bottling and sealing,
before the bubble
on the brink, expands,
takes off.

How there is time
tomorrow
for everything—

everything else,
but this.

REFLECTIONS AT MT COOK

I once wrote that everything
was thank you.
That is not all.
Everything above is as below.
Everything is, in traces,
and at times in your face
fully obvious,
utterly, completely transparent.

Everything is undone
in the way
the sun sparkles on water,
reflects off snow.
In the way there are few colours
but blue and white,
green and brown.
Lake, mountain, snow.

I once noticed everything said
thank you.

Here though,
everything is explanatory.
No need for thank you.
This is the pinnacle,
which in the end is entirely simple.
It is not creation saying thank you,
so much as creation's revelation here
which we are thankful for.

We leave knowing
we have encountered the brink,
that hardly knows,
in a terrain of rockfall and ice,
and open plains,
that we, small dots on the horizon,
made landfall.

And that is how we leave it.
Unmoved and ever existent
despite us.
Everything is thank you,
yes,
and nothing less.
But everything is also as it is.

And it is we,
impermanent in ourselves,
wending our way back,
making our afternoon shadows
on the hills,

becoming smaller and smaller—
as sediment in a mountain stream,
or stones on a valley floor—
who say thank you.

This is the silence
that speaks—so very little,
that only insects are heard.
And what is thank you in the end
but an acknowledgment of our smallness
in the face of everything?
Its vastness the very mirror
that keeps us from our own self-importance.

The mountain hardly knows
its rocks which fall
as stars through the aeons.
The star dust that is our true heritage
is the same as the rock
that claims it is still mountain.

But still looks up,
aware of it being so miniscule
in the face of its forebears.
Yes, so much in need of thank you
are we, so small,
where the mountain peaks
reach heaven.

The work of the eyes is done.
Go now and do the heart-work on the images imprisoned within you.

— Rainer Maria Rilke

FIRE AND ICE

And here is the world.
All fire and ice.
Both inviting and cold.
We stand on the hill
and she blows through us,
a leaf in the wind.
And yet, sets her rainbow
above the route we're to travel.
Sends her plumes of cloud
into the sky,
knowing we'll notice.
She is the ambivalent lover
looking over her shoulder,
sensing us following.
And how can we not,
the way she looks,
the way she makes us feel
when chasing her,
all burning longing.
And how she takes our hands
in the end, smiling
as she leads us into calm harbour.
Yes, the world is a bit like that.
Like what they say about the sea.
How we're to honour it.
To love it, but be a little awestruck,
not turn our backs.
And perhaps
that's what it's all about.

Loving something
that's a little too beautiful to be true—
in that it isn't.
And she, so terribly lovely
and unbearably distant,
that we stand staring from boat's rails
seeing her pass too quickly.
Next time we'll stay longer, we say.
And then we arrive and she's
there shining in the roses
while we're looking at the moon,
thinking we are too far apart.
Ha, we say, we shall pick
you and place you, a flower in a vase
at our bedsides.
So I will die, she says—and smiles.

AT THE HEART

Everything at its heart is a circle.
Everything made to join at the bend,
to reach closure.
Everything is a circle,
so that we ride upon
the motion.
What does tomorrow bring?
We just begin, like a stone rolling.
And where does it end?
We need not fear dissolving,
for even soap bubbles are circles.
Popping and landing, splash in the sink,
to form more bubbles.
There is no end to the rolling movement
of the world and its universe,
the seasons.
And our stories. Each of us a Chapter One,
a Chapter Ten, at the same time.
And as we welcome others in,
we love the continuance in the other.
How we recognise ourselves,
though we might be exiting left.
Someone with our eyes and smile
holds the baton.
Oh, that everything is spiralling
is the most comforting truth in the universe.
Not out of control, as wool unravelling,
but gaining strength

as solar winds, or tidal flows.
I am on the journey, as are you,
we turn to face each other,
and our embrace forms a ring
we're held within.
Anyone who sees time as linear,
or space as pattern-less,
has not closed their eyes to feel
the circling earth,
or wondered at the movements of the sun,
or fallen irreversibly in love,
believing it a gift
to last forever.

MERTON'S CABIN

The grass is green,
the trees overhead,
the meadow flowers
still the same now

as when you lived.
The candle burning
in its holder,
the dust gathering
on the shelf,

the same as you,
with wet cloth,
brushed off.
The wood you cut,
the fire you stoked,
the coffee you set
to brew.

The snow the same,
the waiting for spring,
the counting of the leaves
of fall,
the hearing of the ringing bells
of Lauds.

The rhythms,
the waking

and the falling into sleep.
Everything the same, still,

as then, before my own birth
and first breath,
the hearing of you
speak.

Before I,
now sitting
with one mind straddling
life and death's chasm,
stretch to see you,

and come to understand
all of life, in truth,
as nothing more
than a change of tape
on a recording machine,
as cicada's singing, reborn,

the whistling kettle,
and you with your coat and scarf
over tunic,
having just left the room,

to a path,
once imagined,
and which I now see trodden down
through waving
grasses,

still moving.

Only as a child am I awake
and able to trust
that in every fear and every night
I will behold you again.

However often I get lost,
however far my thinking strays,
I know you will be here, right here,
untouched by time.

— Rainer Maria Rilke

THE SPACE BETWEEN NOTES

So, you want to understand?
What?
The mystery can't be held,
fully conveyed.

Its definition always just a slice
of the whole,
a leaf from a living tree.

And does not every leaf lie unique
in the hand,
an individual web of veins,
colours, design?

So we try to understand,
while each of us draws
from wells of varying expression.

Just like this universe
of an infinite variety
of stars and planets,

in which our own globe hangs
suspended,
at home in the solar winds.

Cellist Yo-yo Ma points
to the space between notes
within which the music occurs.

And I see

how we compose our poems,
make our works of art,
perform our songs,

knowing all along
what is transferred and responded to,
lies somewhere out beyond.

Each reaction just a mix of substances,
made up of who we are
and from whence we've come.

The listening, the reading, the seeing,
our own personal communion
with this mystery to which we belong.

This mystery in the middle,
in the pauses that speak volumes.
The truth that lies untouched
with us dancing at its edge,

words and notes insufficient,
our perspectives drawing vague reflections,
despite the depths of our vision.

We are a people who have climbed
the hill to see the view,
awed by the understanding that beyond
the edges of our sight, lies more.

Humbled, we are anchored to the hill
with our limits of vision,
while perceiving how the awareness

even of mystery
and living open,
is the suspending agent.

Listening for the sounds between
the notes,
hearing the stories of our neighbours,
letting it all sink

as a nameless stone in the soul—
which become the questions we each live into
and the answers too.

There is the music of Heaven in all things.

— Hildegard of Bingen

About the Author

Ana Lisa de Jong is a contemplative poet and published author of nine poetry collections. Ana Lisa's evocative poetry is born of the flora and fauna and unique landscapes of Aotearoa-New Zealand, and a deep, earthy faith. Drawing upon her Celtic and Māori heritage, Ana Lisa responds to the world around us as innately alive and with stories to tell, which she weaves into poems rich in imagery and spiritual insights. Writing prolifically and sensitively, Ana Lisa's grace-imbued words speak deeply to our human condition, both in relationship with one another and as tangata-whenua (people of the land), and many readers find her words a refreshing and hope-filled well of spiritual nourishment. She writes at livingtreepoetry.com and can be found regularly engaging with readers on her Facebook page.

www.ingramcontent.com/pod-product-compliance
Lightning Source LLC
Chambersburg PA
CBHW041432300426
44117CB00001B/1